D1001037

Bill Horan's

MILITARY MODELLING MASTERCLASS

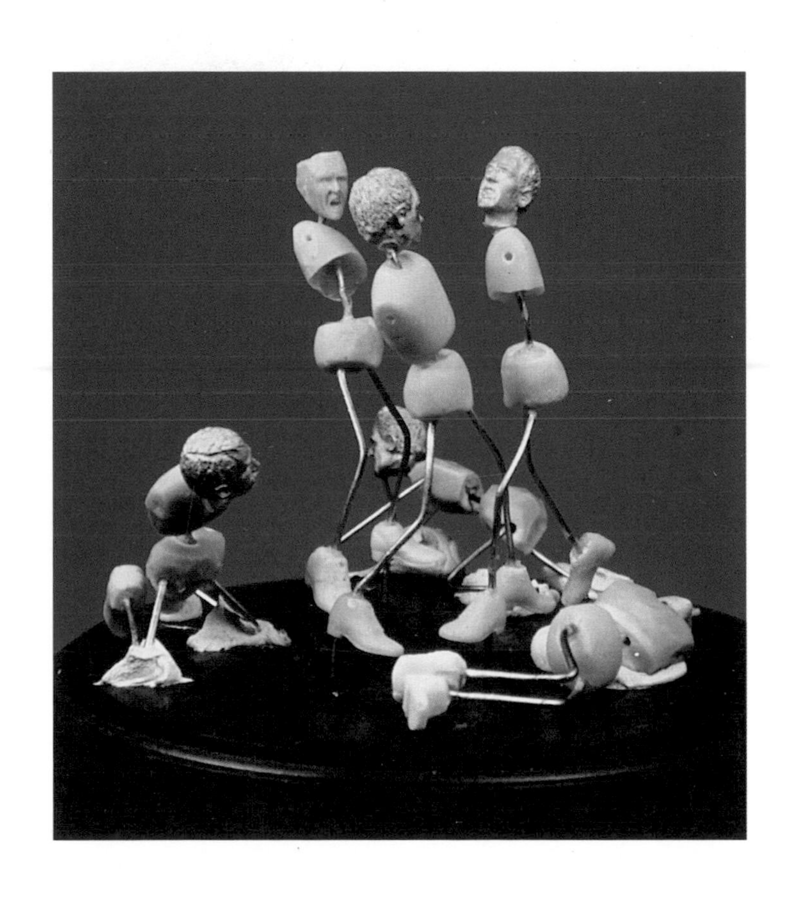

Bill Horan's

MILITARY MODELLING MASTERCLASS

Bill Horan

Windrow & Greene

This edition published in
Great Britain 1994 by
Windrow & Greene Ltd.
19A Floral Street
London WC2E 9DS

Printed in China
Designed by John Anastasio/Creative Line

A CIP catalogue record for this book
is available from the British Library

ISBN 1-872004-09-1

Dedication: To the late Rick Scollins

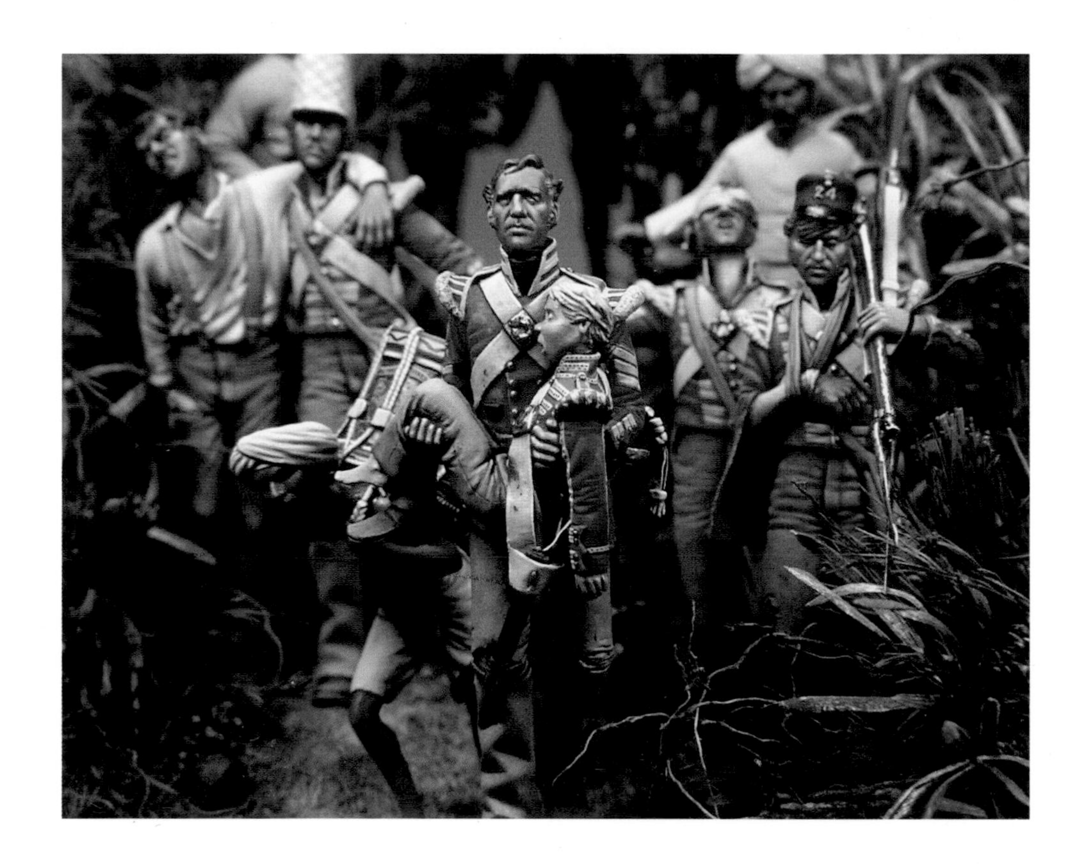

CONTENTS

PREFACE

One day in the spring of 1973 a nervous 14-year-old boy slowly opened the door of the American Eagles hobby shop in Seattle, Washington. Under his arm was a shoebox containing several plastic models, including a Tamiya Kubelwagen complete with a driver and two German staff officers. The models were to be entered in a contest - his first - advertised by the hobby shop, with prizes in the form of gift certificates redeemable at the shop.

As the youngster carefully removed each piece from the shoebox, the proprietor placed them in a glass case alongside the few other models entered thus far. The boy stepped back to admire his work. Both the vehicle and figures were well painted, he thought; the faces were painted à rosy shade of flesh colour, and every part of the uniforms was painted in the colour depicted on the box art. He was especially proud of the glossy finish of the leather waistbelts and boots; and of the eyes - tiny black dots inside the somewhat larger white dots - tough to do with a toothpick, his preferred tool for detail painting.

His father was happy to let the boy browse awhile; and one kit that particularly caught his eye was a Monogram Sherman tank. Noticing that the plastic shrink-wrap was already removed, he slowly opened the kit to have a look inside. On top of the plastic sprues was an 8½in. x 11in. card printed in colour; and as he looked at it his heart sank.

Just a moment earlier his models had looked so marvelous, but a single glance at the card told him just how much he still had to learn. The card carried a brief article by someone named Sheperd Paine, explaining how he had built a dazzlingly realistic diorama with the Sherman kit, complete with figures that were so lifelike they seemed to jump out of the pictures.

My first instinct (because the 14-year-old was, of course, me) was to consider taking up some alternative hobby: like stamp collecting, say, or maybe needlepoint. How could I ever come even close to such perfection? After a while I decided that I really didn't care that much for stamps, and needlepoint frankly sounded too much like a girl's hobby. I determined to stick with model-making - and particularly with miniature figures, which in Sheperd Paine's photos were not the monochromatic mannequins I had painted, but animated, lifelike "mini-people" who caught and held my attention.

A month or so later, as my family was about to relocate to the Far East for several years, I heard that I had won the competition at American Eagles. That was the good news: the bad news was that only one other modeller had entered! It didn't make much difference anyway, as I wasn't able to get back to pick up the award before I left town; and by the time I returned to Seattle three years later, nobody could remember what had happened to that award, or for that matter, who I was. There's probably a lesson in there somewhere...

The purpose of this book is to describe the methods, materials and approach which this particular miniaturist employs in creating stock figures, conversions, vignettes and dioramas. By no means are the techniques described in this book the only way, and there is no one "right" way; they are an assortment of techniques borrowed from many other miniaturists and adapted to my own way of working, together with a few which are uniquely my own.

In addition to describing my own approach to the various miniature subjects with which I am most familiar, I have tried to show, through the many photographs throughout this book, a variety of other methods used by such renowned miniaturists as Peter Twist, Greg DiFranco, Andrei Koribanics, Derek Hansen, Jim Johnston, Phil Kessling, Mike Good, Michel Saez, and many others. Each of these accomplished artists has his own story to tell, and the photos and captions describing their work provide glimpses of other paths available to the miniaturist in search of the techniques most to his or her own liking.

All miniaturists would like to think of themselves as innovators, opening new modelling frontiers and leaving their own indelible stamp on this hobby we all enjoy so much. And while all miniaturists produce work that is truly unique, their techniques are a strange combination of borrowed methods, modified approaches lifted from the pages of "How to" articles (often misunderstood!), and a few original ideas which may or may not make sense to anyone else. However, the techniques are only a part, and not the most important, of the road to success in this hobby.

The constant desire to improve and excel, and a determination to work tirelessly to achieve success are of far greater importance. Success demands a sound armoury of techniques coupled with many, many hours of practice. There are no secret passports to easy success, no step-by-step guides to a gold medal at a prestigious competition. The best modellers are constantly looking for ways of improving the quality of their work, and are never wholly satisfied with their results no matter how many hours of eye-strain and back-ache they have invested. "The face is too pink", they mutter to themselves; "I should have painted some veins on the back of that hand"; "the horse highlighting is too subtle"; "the eyes are too close together (or show too much white - or too little")... and on and on. One might think that receiving awards and compliments from ones peers would bring greater satisfaction with ones work; but while such positive reinforcement is welcome, it never quite sates the desire to do better. Nor should it. A miniaturist's toughest critic should always be himself. Sound principles and many hours of hard work are the common attributes of the most successful miniaturists - and the Grand Masters.

CHAPTER 1

PAINTING A STOCK FIGURE

The most important decision a modeller makes when embarking on the painting of a stock figure is made well before the selection of a hobby knife, a suitable primer, a preferred paint medium, or a dazzling hardwood base. The most important decision is the choice of which figure he will paint. As many modellers are lured to favourite historical periods or fantasy subjects, these same preferences can blind them to flaws in a particular figure that cannot be overcome with a paint brush. The best painters recognize the importance of selecting only the best castings for painting.

The fact that the number of figures currently available to the modeller is truly staggering, running into the hundreds of thousands, makes the decision even more difficult. While there are many excellent figures available on the market, there are even more with disproportionate limbs and hands, squat legs, eyes impossibly close together, mismatched castings, out-of-scale accoutrements, and an assortment of other woeful handicaps that no amount of painting artistry can mask. It is a sad fact that even the most brilliant painting of a bad figure can ultimately result in nothing better than a brilliantly-painted bad figure. Why not simply invest the same skill and effort to produce a brilliantly-painted *excellent* figure?

Selecting the "best" figure certainly does not mean the most expensive. Fine figures can be found among the least as well as the most expensive price ranges. The best way to select one is to study as wide a choice of figures as possible. Look at the face: are the eyes well sculpted and engaging? Are they spaced properly? Is the anatomy properly proportioned? Are the weapons and equipment well designed, correctly scaled and cleanly cast?

The best place to study the many available kits is your local hobby shop, if you are lucky enough to have one. If not, spend some time at the trade stand of a major kit dealer at a model figure show. Ask the proprietor what figures he recommends within your favourite period, and study them. Of course, the most obvious people to ask are other modellers; chances are you will stumble onto someone who has painted the figure you are contemplating, and you might get some helpful insight into its strengths and weaknesses.

The figure I have chosen for this exercise is David Grieve's excellent 100mm Sergeant, 79th Regiment of Foot (Highlanders), 1815.

The David Grieve 100mm figure of a Sergeant of the 79th (Cameron) Highlanders, 1815. The mold seams have all been removed and the figure is partially assembled, ready for priming.

PREPARATIONS

As any good model assembly instruction guide will tell you, the first step that should always be taken is to carefully wash all the parts to remove any chemicals that may remain from the molding process, and then to check the fit of all the parts. I must confess right away that I have never washed a figure. It's probably a good bit of advice, but one I have never taken very seriously; and I cannot ever recall an instance where I primed a figure, had the paint peel off, and said to myself, "Darn, I KNEW I should have washed that figure!"

Checking the fit of parts is important - not so much the fit of arms and head, as these must be attached anyway and any gaps, large or small, must be filled before the figure can be primed. It is the equipment and weapons that often require assembly in a specific order, which if not followed can lead to serious problems later on, and sometimes to reworking. For example, one may find that a canteen strap will only fit

(Above) An even coat of Floquil spray primer has been applied to the figure, and allowed to dry for 24 hours before undercoating commences.

(Above right) Close-up of the head and upper body prior to undercoating. A high-quality casting and a thin, even primer coat leave all the fine details sharp.

in place if attached before attachment of the left arm. Take it from one who has made this type of mistake repeatedly over the years - test-fit the parts!

A whole assortment of tools are available to remove the mold lines from a figure: hobby knives, emery paper, files of all shapes and sizes, and steel (wire) wool. While I have made use of all these at one time or another, by far the most useful tool of the bunch is the hobby knife. By using a gentle scraping motion, virtually all mold lines can be removed from metal, resin or plastic. In areas where the scraping has flattened out an area unnaturally I like to go back and smooth it out with emery paper (super fine sandpaper), or a file. Areas where the surface is unusually rough often require a good buffing with steel wool. Cleaning up a figure can take anywhere from 30 minutes to eight hours, depending on the complexity of the figure and the quality of the casting.

Once the parts have been prepared and checked for fit it's time to start assembly. Like most modellers, I use a quick-drying epoxy glue for assembling metal parts. The bond created is very strong, more durable than with other types of cements, including "superglue" (though this works very well with resin figures). If well designed, the casting will require very little filling around the arm joints; in fact, the epoxy forced out when pressing the arms into place can be smeared around the joint, providing a quick and effective filling for minor gaps.

Larger gaps will require some putty work. Virtually any type of putty can be used for this purpose, and I usually use A&B Epoxy. It blends into the adjoining surfaces smoothly, and dries to a rock-hard consistency, making it ideal for filing.

There are many modellers who strongly believe that the entire figure should always be assembled prior to painting; their brave credo is "If you can see it, you can paint it." While this is often undeniably true, so too there are many cases when it simply is not. While most things that can be seen can be accessed with a brush of some sort, it does not necessarily follow that all such

areas can be painted with the care their visibility requires.

For example, the backpack for the figure being painted here has a hollow square on the inside. Once attached, the inside of this square could be seen very clearly at oblique angles; yet getting a paint brush into that area would be virtually impossible. Similarly, the crossbelts and straps beneath the pack would be extremely difficult to reach in such a way as to shade and highlight them with the desired care. Areas around the haversack, sash and canteen fall into the same category of "easy to see, not so easy to paint". When the goal is to produce the best painted figure possible, details like these require a bit more attention than might normally be expected. Only the arms were glued onto our subject figure prior to priming. Each equipment item was cleaned up, primed and painted separately.

The last step necessary prior to priming of the figure is pinning. The small pins typically located under the heels of most figures are not adequate to support the weight of a metal figure, and additional reinforcement is needed. Those who have decided that this is not necessary, only to find their carefully painted but

(Above left) Bonnet, face, stock and collar are undercoated in the basic colours in which they are to be finished. After setting up for five to six hours, this undercoat served to prevent the blending processes from accidentally exposing the grey primer on heavily-worked areas.

(Above) The checkered band of the Highland bonnet in the course of painting with vertical stripes and a single central horizontal stripe of red. Green squares are painted over the intersections of the red stripes.

poorly pinned figure rolling loosely around the inside of the transport box after arrival at a figure show, can attest to the wisdom of this additional precaution.

First, carve off the existing pins. Next, drill two holes in the heels wide enough to accommodate the selected pins. I typically use $^{1}/_{8}$in. x 2in. nails with the heads nipped off, but piano wire or even heavy duty paper clip wire can work as well - the latter is ideal for 54mm figure pinning. The hole should go at least $^{1}/_{2}$in. into the heel, or further depending on the weight distribution of the figure. Between $^{3}/_{4}$in. and 1in. should extend from the bottom of the heel to go into the base. Both heels so pinned should provide a reliable attachment.

Once the figure has been attached to the working base (I use a rough wooden block), the figure is primed using a can of Floquil Grey Spray Primer. The Floquil spray seals the metal very nicely and provides a good, dead matt surface that holds the paint well. The Floquil primer needs at least 24 hours to dry, which is best accomplished in a warm, dry place. I have even left figures in the oven overnight at 140 degrees Fahrenheit to hasten the process.

Once the figure has been primed, it is always a good idea to examine it closely one more time for any mold lines or casting imperfections that may have been missed at the clean-up stage. Invariably I find some flaw that must be dealt with.

PAINTING

I paint almost exclusively with Humbrol enamel paints. It would be nice to say that this was a conscious decision based on a careful evaluation of the many painting mediums available. Unfortunately the truth is not nearly so impressive. As a young modeller I got into the habit of buying my paints at the hobby shop where I bought my models and, not having access to any other information, assumed that all other painters did the same. By the time I realized that artist's oils were the most commonly used medium I had already developed an enamel-painting technique with which I was comfortable.

The greatest benefit of enamels is their dead matt realism, a quality that makes them ideal not only for recreating realistic fabric colours, but also for weathering. Uniform and equipment details that require a bit of a sheen need only be coated with a clear gloss, or a semi-gloss mixture of clear flat and gloss paints.

The short drying time of enamels is often bemoaned by oil painters. Actually, enamels can be blended very well for a period of 25-35 minutes after application. By keeping colour mixtures simple, and working in relatively small areas one at a time, there is ample time for careful blending of colours.

Actually, the shorter drying time can be a blessing in disguise. While it is true that the longer blending time of oils allows more time for experimenting, the temptation to "overblend" - working mid-tones, highlights and shadow colours into a single nondescript shade - is too much for many oil painters.

A word is in order here concerning brushes. There are a wide array of fine brushes available to artists on the market, including many of the red sable variety. While I certainly cannot claim to have tried them all, I have tried enough to know that Winsor & Newton Series 7 red sable brushes are simply superb for detail painting. While I listen politely at trade stands to salesmen hawking their "as-good-as-Winsor & Newton-and-much-cheaper" brushes, I can never forget my many frustrating experiments with imitations. Series 7 brushes are indeed expensive, but they are certainly worth the money. I can't think of a single top painter who doesn't use them.

Once the primer has dried thoroughly, each of the primary areas to be painted is undercoated in the base

(Top left) The initial application of the lightest shadow colour to the face, prior to blending. Note the location of the areas of shadow. It all looks straightforward enough at this stage, in this enlarged photo; but this head is actually the size of a fingernail. Patience is essential to achieving the necessary precision.

(Bottom left) A medium shadow colour is added to the centre of most of the areas of light shadow. This colour is focused in the deepest part of the cheek hollow, the folds between the corners of the mouth and the nose, and around the eyes. The edges of the medium shadow are then blended into the light shadow.

(Top right) The light shadow is carefully blended into the base colour at the edges only; the distinction between base and shadow colours must remain evident after the transitional areas are subtly blurred.

(Bottom right) The final dark shadow is applied to the deepest recesses of the face - those areas most concealed from the imaginary light source - and the edges are once again blended into the medium shadow colour.

colour. For example, the face is painted flesh colour, the bonnet band white, feathers black, coatee red. This will provide a foundation for the blending soon to begin, and ensure that any areas requiring heavy brush work do not expose the grey primer. I allow about four to six hours for this coat to dry, and usually try to apply the base coats just before leaving to go to work, or at night.

PAINTING THE FACE

I always start by painting the face. There are practical as well as psychological reasons for this. Painting "from the inside out" minimizes the risk of accidentally slopping paint over outer areas while trying to paint inner ones. But the main reason for painting the face first is its overall importance to the figure's appearance. The face is without question the most important feature on any figure (except, perhaps, a knight wearing a closed helmet...). I find that if the face goes well, I become energized to work through the less glamorous aspects of painting the figure (like knapsacks and sword slings). To get the face right is to overcome the biggest challenge to producing a well-painted figure.

First the face is given a thin coat of a flesh mixture. I like to use a combination of Humbrol Flesh, Natural Wood, Scarlet and a bit of Leather. The ratios of each of these components vary greatly depending on the complexion of the figure I am depicting. Most soldiers spend an enormous amount of time in the open air, and

(Left) The first highlight colour is added.

(Above) After the blending of the edges of the initial highlights, a final extra light highlight is sparingly applied to "pull out" the facial features - the corner of the cheekbone, the undulations in the nose, the top of the chin, and areas above the upper lip; the ear will also receive this treatment. At this point the shaping of the eyes and the painting of the teeth, lips and tongue were also completed.

photos of soldiers on campaign invariably show them with what we would today call a great tan. Even the venerable Robert E. Lee's face appears to be quite brown in several of the photographs taken of him during the American Civil War. For this reason, I usually add more brown and red colours and less Flesh. This thinned coat of paint is allowed to partially set for about 20 minutes before the shading begins.

The first shadow colour applied is the subtlest one, using a mixture similar to that used for the face, but with less Flesh and bit more Leather and red. Once again the mixture is kept very thin - transparent, in fact - and is applied in the hollow under the cheekbones, along the fold beside the nose and on each side of the nose, in the temples, beneath the lower lip, and under the eye bag. After these areas are blocked out, the edges (and only the edges) are carefully blended into the base colour using a very gentle stroking/stippling motion. The intent here is to pull the two colours together along the "border" so that one seems to fade into the other. Great care is taken to ensure that two distinctively coloured areas remain, each fading into the other, and not a single colour made from a combination of the two.

The same basic process is now repeated over a smaller area with a slightly darker version of the shadow mixture, this time made by mixing Leather, red and a bit of black to produce a medium chocolate colour with a slightly reddish tinge. This darker "intermediate" shadow colour is applied in the upper portion of the cheek hollow, inside the folds beside the nose, between the lips, under the nose, under the inside portion of the eye bags and the inside half of the hollow above the eye. In each case the intermediate shadow is meant to deepen the shadow effect in these areas, and is applied using the bullseye principle, i.e., progressively smaller darker shadow colours applied within each other.

Finally, a very dark red/black mixture is applied to a few selected areas, such as beneath the nose, in a small portion of the folds beside the nose, and in the eye area. By building gradually from subtle shadows to very dark ones, a bold, dramatic painting effect can be achieved. It is always better to be too bold than too timid. The timid painter, whose shadows and highlights are so subtle as to be virtually indiscernible, often finds his efforts go unnoticed in the glare of display cases and the poor lighting so typical of miniature exhibitions.

The last highlights have received their final blending; eye detailing has been completed; "five o'clock shadow" has been applied in the form of a controlled wash; and the whole face has been given a clear coat of water-based semi-gloss to add a sense of moisture. The bonnet and collar have been finished. Basic colours have been laid down on the coat, lace "loops" and sash; and work on the crossbelt and pack straps is progressing.

Once the shadows have been applied, two layers of highlights are added. I consider the effective use of highlights a critical step, and one often neglected by otherwise good painters. The first highlight colour applied, for which I use a mixture of Flesh with a bit of red, Natural Wood and white, should be clearly lighter than the base colour, and compatible in tone. In other words, a base colour with a reddish tinge to it must have a similar tinge in the highlights; a more heavily tanned face may have had more Leather in the base coat; and these factors must be considered when mixing the suitable highlight shade.

Highlights are applied to the cheekbones, the bone above the eyebrows, the bridge of the nose, the nostrils, the top of the chin, above the upper lip, at the top of the eye bag, and along the diagonal ridge going from the inner eye towards the corner of the jaw. Each highlight is carefully blended into the adjoining colour.

The second highlight is much lighter in colour, and is intended to pinpoint certain areas most likely to reflect light. The point of the cheekbones, the tip of the nose (and sometimes the "break" in the nose), the area just below the folds beside the nose, and the top of the chin are each highlighted, taking care to ensure that the application is confined to a small portion of each area. The highlight is then blended into the base colour.

The next step is the eyes. Starting with the "whites", which of course are not white at all, a mixture of white and Natural Wood is applied in a wedge shape to each eye. Next a carefully painted line, following the shape of the eye, is applied to the upper portion of the eye. Along the lower edge of the eye a thin line is drawn using the light shadow colour used on the face. Once the eye is thus defined, the eyeball is painted using a medium blue colour, care being taken to ensure that the colour fills about 80% of the eye with only very small areas of "white" left showing on each side. The greater size of the 100mm figure allows for more detail in the eye painting than a 54mm figure, and I like to add a small black dot to the pupil; as a final touch, a tiny dot of sky blue is carefully applied to each side of the upper portion of the eyeball, to add a bit of a "twinkle".

Eyebrows are painted with a dark brown mixture, the shape being thicker near the middle of the forehead, fading and thinning as they tail away towards the temple. A thin black underline beneath the thickest portion of the eyebrow adds depth to them, and a few carefully applied highlights complete the effect.

As most soldiers on campaign don't have time to shave every day, a "five o'clock shadow" is almost a must. A combination of black and Flesh is used to create a charcoal grey colour. This mixture must be kept very thin while it is applied to the whisker areas. While the paint is still wet the edges are blended, and highlighted areas are cleared out so that only a slight hint of the grey colour is evident there.

The neck, ears and hair are painted separately using the same principles described for the face. Highlighting is particularly important for the ears, the top edge and the inner protrusions receiving special attention.

As a final touch, a thin coat of water-based Polly S semi-gloss is applied to the entire face and neck area (as it will be later to the hands and knees). The semi-gloss is created by mixing more or less equal portions of clear gloss and clear flat paints, and brings added depth and a sense of moisture to the skin. I consider this step to be an absolute must for enamel painters, and only after completing it do I ever feel that the face is truly finished.

PAINTING THE REST OF THE FIGURE

Once the head has been completed, the rest of the figure is painted working from the top downwards,

(Right) The upper part of the body, sleeves and hands have been completed (note careful shadowing and highlighting on the hands, particularly). Now the basic colours have been laid down on the kilt, with broad green stripes painted at regular vertical and horizontal intervals over a base coat of dark blue.

(Far right) The completed 79th Highlander's kilt in Cameron of Erracht tartan. Note the dark overall appearance, and the subdued tones of the fine red and yellow lines except where the yellow-on-yellow intersections make spots of bright colour.

painting each area from the inside out. The bonnet band was first undercoated in an off-white mixture of white, with small amounts of black and Natural Wood colours. The top edge of the band was carefully edged with a thin pure white line to separate it from the body of the bonnet. This principle will be used throughout the painting of the figure's uniform and equipment. The red checks were added next with another subdued mixture, this time a red diluted with a bit of Natural Wood and Flesh to suggest fading. Where the red vertical and horizontal lines crossed, a dark green square was painted. Precision is the key to successfully painting the bonnet band. It is also very important that a good sharp detail brush be used, such as a 000.

The bonnet feathers were undercoated with a mixture of Humbrol Black and a bit of Winsor & Newton artist oil Lamp Black. The oil paint helps to give the black more depth, thereby allowing for more subtlety in the highlighting. Highlights were carefully applied line by line using two shades of blue-grey. The base highlight was a dark blue-grey colour, with a lightened version in certain raised areas, and along the edges of the feathers. I NEVER dry-brush feathers, as the crude against-the-grain look inherent to that technique runs counter to the soft graceful effect desired for the feathers. In fact I try to stay away from dry-brushing in general as much as possible.

The coatee and the equipment were painted from the inside out once again, starting with the collar, then the jacket, lace/buttons, sash, crossbelts, shoulder straps/tuft and finally buckles and plate. The techniques used in the painting of each area are identical to those used in painting the face; the initial application of a thin base coat, followed by three progressively darker shadow tones, and one to two shades of highlight, each application feathered into the adjoining colour using a brush slightly moistened with thinner. To maintain the warmth of the red throughout the shaded areas, a bit of Alizarin Crimson oil paint was used with the Humbrol Scarlet (60), over a base coat mixed from Scarlet, Leather and Brick Red. Flesh was added to this base colour to create the highlight colour. Flesh adds a convincing dusty, faded look to the red.

The white lace and belts were painted with the same principle used for the bonnet band; white/black/Natural Wood off-white mixture highlighted with pure white and shaded with a darker version of the base colour. The crimson sash was painted with a base colour of German Purple (70), Scarlet (60) and Alizarin Crimson oil paint. The shadow colour is Alizarin Crimson, Scarlet and black, while the highlights were created by adding bit of Flesh to the base mixture. A generic dark green was used for the central stripe. The woollen tufts at the ends of the shoulder straps were first painted a pale brownish grey colour, then "dabbed" (not dry-brushed) with progressively lighter highlights, the last being pure white.

It is worth noting that the canteen was painted separately, the steel retaining bands being painted blue along with the wooden portions. The fact that no paint remains on the metal bands on extant canteens has led some to mistakenly report that the steel bands were left a bright steel colour. In fact, the entire canteen was given an overall coat of paint after assembly, bands and all.

All buckles were painted (and highlighted/ shaded) either with a yellow ochre mixture coated with a gloss finish, or with silver printer's ink mixed with gloss black enamel paint. I like to use the ochre (Humbrol Yellow, Leather and Burnt Umber oil paint), as it facilitates more precise highlighting and shading than the metallics without the "grainy" appearance.

PAINTING THE KILT AND HOSE

Painting a kilt is a challenge that many find extremely intimidating, and there are good reasons for that. Good kilt painting does indeed involve several overlaid colours, many straight, narrow lines and a great deal of precision. However, many of these challenges may be overcome with some simple planning.

The Cameron of Erracht kilt (one of the more complicated) was first over-painted with a dark blue colour. Once thoroughly dry, dark green bands were painted at regular intervals horizontally and vertically around the kilt, care being taken to ensure that they

(Below) Note the tight pleating of the rear of the kilt, where the muted black lines edging the green bands show clearly. The rear of the jacket shows highlighting and shadowing to visually "pull out" or "push back" the different areas of cloth around the pocket, turnback, rear pleat, lower edge. etc. The aspiring medal-winner must discipline himself to give the same patient attention to the less glamorous items, such as the knapsack.

(Above & above right) The knapsack and water canteen were attached to a temporary base with Pres-Stik and painted separately for later attachment to the figure.

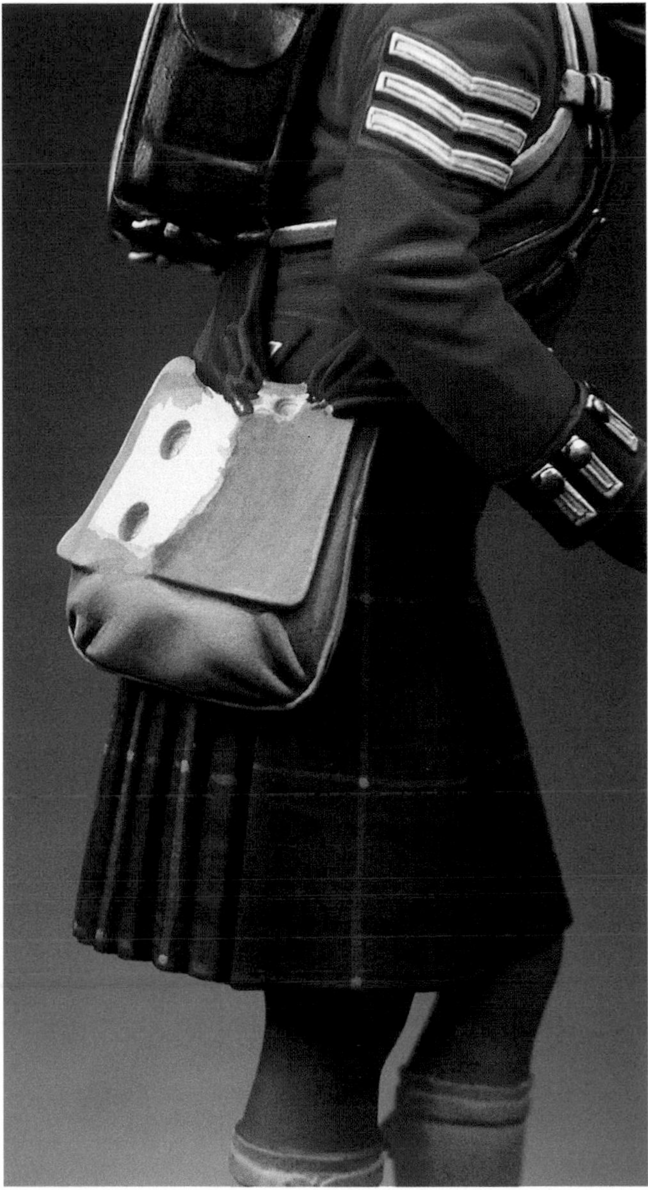

(Right) The haversack and right hip area, painted and ready for the attachment of the separately painted sash end and canteen. Note the lace and button detail. This mercilessly over-lifesize enlargement (remember - the whole figure is only about 4ins. high) does emphasize the shadow work around the edges of cuffs, equipment straps, etc.

were as even as possible. Once dry, black bordering lines were painted along the edges of each green band. Now the fun begins!

The Cameron tartan involves groups of four red lines running along each row of the pattern (a good tartan reference book was consulted for the grouping of these lines), with a single yellow line running down only the green bands. The key to mixing these colours is to keep them very dark. The red colour is actually a dark reddish brown, while the yellow is a deep yellowish green. Keep in mind that the red and yellow fabric is intermingled on the kilt with the colour fabric beneath it. Hence, the yellow and red threads are equally intermingled with green or blue threads. Mixing green/blue into the red and yellow will produce an effect very much like that visible on the actual tartan.

The trickiest step in painting the lines is keeping them even, straight and narrow. There is no magic trick to this, just practice and patience. Don't expect to find a convenient can of tartan spray paint at your local hobby shop! All detail painting such as this is accomplished by carefully and securely bracing the arm/hand holding the figure and the brush. The paint on the brush must be kept thin enough to flow smoothly from the brush in an even line. Obviously, a good sharp detail brush is an essential here.

When all lines are complete, a final touch is a speck of pure yellow where the yellow lines cross. In these tiny areas the threads are pure yellow, hence the subdued colours desired for the rest of the lines are not applicable.

Once the tartan is painted, it's a good idea to step back and look at it critically. Tartans should be very dark in appearance. If the reds and yellow (or even the blue and green bands) appear too bright, as they did to me in this case, a thin wash of Winsor & Newton Blue/Black was applied to subtly deepen the colour. Great care must be taken not to make it too dark, but this step also brings a unity to the finish which will add an extra degree of realism.

The hose were painted using the same principles as those used on the kilt, with the exception that the pinkish bands were painted diagonally. Where they cross, a red diamond was painted. In examining Highland hose, one can see that the pink areas are not actually pink, but have a red and white speckled appearance. This was duplicated by adding a scattering of red and white flecks to these pink areas.

Getting the pink bands to meet in the back of the hose can be a real problem, but this was solved by simply painting a light grey "seam" up the back of the hose, and terminating each band at that line. That is, after all, how the hose are designed, so it has the added benefit of being realistic, as well as expedient.

A word is in order here concerning paint medium for

this type of painting. Very few oil painters use oil colours for tartan work, as the shiny finish tends to look unrealistic, while the thinner consistency of the oil paint makes it more difficult to paint even, opaque lines. If enamels are a problem for you, most water-based acrylic paints are also well suited to tartan work.

GROUNDWORK & FINISHING TOUCHES

I selected a finely turned Bolivian rosewood base for the figure, approximately 2ins. in height. The added height sets off the figure and helps to draw attention, while the exquisite finish of the base brings an air of elegance to its display. There are few images more discouraging in this hobby than a well painted figure mounted on a cheap, poorly finished base. If one is going to put many hours into carefully painting a miniature to be shown to friends, family and peers within the hobby, it makes sense to present it as handsomely as it deserves. There are so many ready-made bases available nowadays that there really is no excuse for cutting corners on this important element.

Holes were drilled into the base to accommodate the locating pins in the heels of the figure, into which the figure was trial-fitted. The figure was then removed, and paperclip wires were stuck into the holes to establish their location while A&B putty was worked over the base to form the shape of the groundwork. I like to use putty for small areas requiring groundwork, due to its "moldability", and the fact that it forms a very firm foundation to which the figure's feet can be glued.

Once the shape of the terrain was established, small pebbles were embedded in the groundwork, and a combination of dirt and baking soda was sprinkled over it. Finally, the entire surface was textured by pressing a rough stone into the putty to create a coarse, uneven texture to the "soil". The entire process took fifteen minutes, after which the figure was placed under a warm lamp for an hour to dry (the oven can crack the finish on the wooden base).

The soil and rocks were painted with enamels, with limited *light* dry-brushing, coupled with washes of Burnt Umber oil paint to create varying shades for the soil. Static grass was attached in clumps using white glue, after which it was painted a dull yellowish brown colour. The final touch was the nameplate, made by special order at a local trophy shop.

* * *

The true key to painting stock figures is to pay proper attention to the details. While careful blending and shading are very important, each aspect of the figure should be given the full attention it deserves, whether that means taking care not to "slop" one colour over into an adjoining one, or to paint a subtle wood grain into the canteen. Don't ask yourself "will anyone else notice?" *You* will notice; and satisfying yourself that you have done everything possible to make the figure appealing to both the casual and the searching eye will bring a much greater sense of accomplishment.

(Above left) The first pink diagonal bands are painted on the hose, a process that will be repeated in the opposite direction; the intersecting diamonds will then be painted a pure red colour, and the hose finished with red/ white flecking to simulate the effect of the original knitting.

(Left) Groundwork has been formed with A&B putty; the base should previously be drilled to take the pins on the figure's feet, the holes being guarded with wires or toothpicks while the groundwork is built up. Here a rough stone is pressed into the still-moist putty to add contour and texture.

(Above) The canteen, sash end and half-pike have been added.

(Right) The David Grieve 100mm 79th Highlander figure completely painted and mounted.

(Left) Drab uniforms need not necessarily make drab figures. The author's Roll Call Miniatures figure of an officer of the 10th Hussars in India in 1880 was brought to life with a carefully painted face, and a variety of deep and light earth tones to add life to the khaki tunic.

(Left) A distinctive face-painting style, which gives his miniatures an expression of stern determination, is one of the conspicuous features of *Jim Ryan's* oil painting technique. Note also the masterly treatment of the "tiger stripe" uniform; camouflage clothing offers a true challenge to the figure painter. Obviously, a good reference source and a lot of patient practice are essential first steps. Shading can be a particular problem. Many miniaturists simply apply dark washes in the folds of the clothing after the painted camouflage design has dried. Far more difficult is the technique used here with such success by Ryan - shading the different colours in the design at each step of the process.

(Right) *Don Weeks* is among the best of today's stock figure painters. He brings to this Chota Sahib kit a well-balanced mixture of sharp detail painting, and the restraint necessary to shade and highlight darker colours convincingly while keeping them looking like dark colours.

(Left) Subtle details can be fun to add, and will enhance the enjoyment of studying a figure. This Conquistador has a face scarred by smallpox; and note the wear and discoloration around the tears in the hose.

(Right) "Flats" present a unique challenge for the painter: a sense of depth and roundness must be created on a virtually flat casting, involving the illusion of a consistent light source. Nearly all flat-painters work in artist oil colours; and few indeed do it better than *Greg DiFranco*, whose superb Kaiser Maximilian is pictured here.

(Right) ***Greg DiFranco's*** **skill in shading the ever-difficult white, and the heavily draped greatcoat, are examples of complicated painting problems solved through careful planning, the laying in of shadow and highlight colours, and tight brushwork in blending them without merging the many shades into a few mid-tones.**

(Left) ***Larry Munne's*** **painting of Stadden's 1980s Parachute Regiment figure - painted as a member of 1 Para - is an excellent study in combat weathering and meticulous camouflage painting. Note how the dusty boots and trousers seem to have absorbed real dust - no superficial dry-brushing here. The effect was achieved by mixing the earth tones into the trouser colour as the figure was painted, not as an afterthought.**

(Left) Adding detail to an otherwise simple kit can pay off. *Mike Good's* painting of an intricate pattern on this Sioux warrior's shirt, coupled with the other well-painted elements, makes for an unexpectedly exciting finish to a basically static figure.

(Right) Napoleonics offer popular opportunities to work with some gorgeous uniform facing colours. Note the excellent handling of both bright and subtly subdued shades in *Keith Kowalski's* French Dragoon officer.

(Right) The details of display are an often overlooked element, which with careful planning can lift a stock figure right out of the ordinary. Elevation invariably draws attention to a figure; *Mike Good* uses height, and materials sympathetic to the subject, to add drama to this 54mm Viking.

(Left) Careful weathering and "distressing" can add interest and dimension to an otherwise simple figure, as in the case of this converted LeCimier casting of a French Fusilier. The head and shako were replaced, and a water gourd added. Note the oil and food stains on the uniform and belts; the free-hanging chinscales on the shako; and the shadow effect inside the tears in the clothing.

(Left) There are few miniaturists capable of making stock kits look like scratch-built vignettes, and *Brian Stewart* is their leader. The Landsknecht's weathered clothing was painted in oils with muted earth tones mixed into the wet paint during the blending process. Stewart is famous for his "ground effects"; note the immaculate handling of the ancient stone fountain. The final touch is the drip of water from the mug in his left hand.

(Below left) Like Mike Good, *Derek Hansen* is well known for his scratch-building skills; but his oil painting of Chota Sahib's officer of the 95th Foot is a textbook example of skilful highlighting and shading coupled with precise detail.
(Photo Derek Hansen)

(Right) Another superb example of the way *Brian Stewart* makes a stock kit tell a story. His Norman mercenary, a Mitrecap casting, is posed amid the wonderfully realised ruins of past wars, turning a face full of character on a reminder of his own all too probable fate.

(Below) *John Canning's* painting of this Hussard du Marais kit of a Celtic chieftain is a good example of the handling of bronze metallic effects - and of the always-difficult painting of blond hair.

(Left) When painting dark blue, "less is more", as in the author's painting of Monarch's US Marine officer. (The moistened end of the cigar took only a moment, but adds realism.)

(Right) There is no easy trick to painting the intricate jewellery of this LeCimier Pharoah Thothmes III, based on an Angus McBride painting; it simply took *Phil Kessling* many hours of tedious, but ultimately satisfying work. The face and limbs are painted to a similarly high standard, making for an impressive figure. *(Photo:Phil Kessling)*

(Left) Often a figure can be remarkably simple in appearance, yet still command attention through its stance, feel for period, clean appearance, or some other understated strength. The author painted this Monarch kit of an officer of German Imperial Marines, 1914, in about eight hours.

(Right) Although a minor conversion, *Adrian Bay's* painting of Capitaine Dampierre of the Chasseurs d'Afrique, 1854, shows the realism that can be achieved with enamels, from the matted look of the clothing to the perfect precision of the sleeve lace and jacket embroidery.

(Left) Among the most accomplished painters in the world, *Michel Saez* of France specializes in "bust" miniatures. His subtle depiction of the skin tones of this Sikh Subadar is a model of restraint and delicate brushwork.
(Photo:Michel Saez)

(Right) A LeCimier kit of a French General of Brigade, 1812, painted by the author. Painting rich gold lacing can be especially rewarding, since it is not nearly as difficult as it looks. The lace on the hat and coat was a mixture of Humbrol Gold, Humbrol Leather and Burnt Umber oil paint. The mixture retains a metallic look, though not the brightness of a pure metallic paint; shading was accomplished with straight Burnt Umber.

(Right) Note the softness of the beard, and the gentle shading of the facial features in this Chasseur d'Afrique bust by *Michel Saez*; the angle of the brow and the glance give this colonial cavalryman an intriguing air of menace.
(Photo:Michel Saez)

(Below) Another superbly oil-painted scratch-built bust by *Michel Saez*, depicting a Zouave of the Imperial Guard at the time of the battle of Magenta, 1859. This Zouave brought home a gold medal from the 1993 World Model Soldier Exposition in Washington DC. *(Photo:Michel Saez)*

(Above) *Ron Tunison* is a true Master when it comes to capturing likenesses; this is his fine rendering of Custer at Little Bighorn. *(Photo:Ron Tunison)*

(Above) In Tunison's "Victory Dance" effective weathering and an animated, superbly war-painted face combine to make a colourful and exciting figure.
(Photo:Ron Tunison)

(Below) Tunison's "No Second Chances"; notice the worn, softened texture of the buckskin shirt and the similar effect in the red-dyed leggings.
(Photo:Ron Tunison)

(Left) *Phil Kessling* glues fine fibre flocking to the sculpted fur of his 54mm figures to add texture and dimension, as seen here in his painting of LeCimier's Desvaux de St.Maurice. Although Phil is primarily an oil painter he uses matt acrylics for dark blues, in place of the glossy-sheened blues available in oil colours.

(Right) Michel Saez designed Metal Modeles' Sioux warrior, painted here by *Jean-Pierre Duthilleul*, one of several French entries to win gold medals at the July 1993 World Model Soldier Exposition, Washington DC. *(Photo:J- P.Duthilleul)*

CHAPTER 2

CONVERTING & CREATING FIGURES

The term "conversion" within the context of the military miniature hobby has a very broad definition. It can be used with equal accuracy to describe anything from the grafting of a new arm - or even just a moustache! - to a stock figure casting, to the creation of a figure built almost entirely from scratch but incorporating a few commercially cast items. This chapter deals with the latter approach.

In spite of the enormous variety of stock figure kits on the market today, many miniaturists are often frustrated at their inability to find exactly the figures they wish to paint - whether from the viewpoint of historical period, nationality, pose, or some other particular personal preference. In my case a fascination for certain historical periods, and particularly for the British Victorian era, bred a desire to paint a broad range of figures from that period. Unfortunately, in the early 1980s relatively few Victorian subjects were commercially available. Out of frustration, I began experimenting with the major conversion of Airfix Multipose figures - a process pioneered by such fine miniaturists as Mike Leonard and Peter Jensen. Over time, my conversion of Multipose figures evolved into a process which, while still utilizing such key commercially available parts as heads, hands and weapons, is closer in spirit to scratch-building than converting. In this chapter I will focus on this process: specifically, on the step-by-step creation of a 54mm Confederate infantryman of the American Civil War.

PREPARATION, TOOLS & MATERIALS

The tools needed to create lifelike 54mm conversions need not be terribly sophisticated; in this, as in so many other crafts, it is not the tools one chooses which are important, but the manner in which one learns to use them. The most important requirement is that the miniaturist understands what tasks he faces, and ensures that he has the appropriate tools to hand. The primary tools which I use in the conversion/scratch-building process are limited to two or three tapered round-section toothpicks, an X-Acto knife, a small piece of emery paper, ultra-fine steel wool, a small pair of pliers, a pair of nippers and a small pair of sharp scissors. The usefulness of all these is self-evident, with the possible exception of the toothpicks.

I prepare these by rolling about 3/8in. at each end of the toothpick in a puddle of superglue and allowing it to dry. The coated surfaces are then lightly sanded, and given a second coat. The superglue forms a non-stick coating on the wood, making it ideal for 54mm sculpting. Further, by carving and sanding the ends of toothpicks I can produce a wide variety of implements for specific sculpting tasks. This most basic workhorse of my sculpting method is thus cheap and easy to make, and if it gets lost or broken it can be replaced in a matter of minutes.

Choosing a material in which to sculpt the

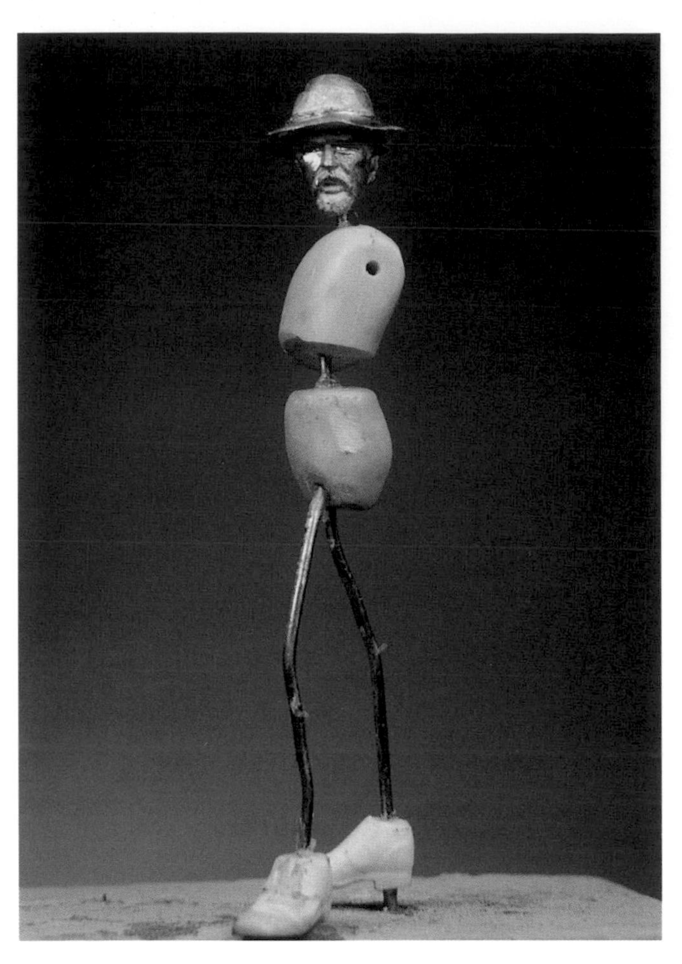

(Left) The basic posing of the figure is critical if the stance is to be convincing. Our Confederate will stand casually with his weight over his slightly backwards-bowed right leg; note the positioning of torso and pelvis, creating an arch in the back. The basic body masses are pre-cast resin components, the head a standard Shenandoah Miniatures part.

(Right) Once the pose had been perfected the legs, waist and neck were solidified with a first roughly applied layer of A&B putty to "lock in" the pose, and provide a foundation for the clothing to be sculpted later. Note the angle of the left leg, and the forward tilt of the head against the arch of the back, giving balance.

figure is a highly subjective decision; it may seem like a bit of a cop-out to say that each modeller should choose whatever works best for him or her, but it is the simple truth. Successful results can be achieved with a vast assortment of putties and other mediums, from auto-body filler to the more classical Sculpey (a traditional modelling clay hardened by baking). I use two principal forms of putty: Duro Epoxy Ribbon, and A&B Epoxy Putty.

The strength of A&B is its best attribute, and it is primarily used for forming the figure armatures; however, I also use it for certain clothing effects where smooth transitions and subtle drapery are required. Many accomplished sculptors swear by A&B for most applications; but in my own view its consistency and relative graininess make it less suitable for the finer detailing needed in 54mm scale. Duro has a soft, waxy working consistency and produces a virtually grainless contour; I use it almost exclusively for clothing, detailing, and most equipment items. A unique feature of Duro is its ability to dry completely when mixed in various ratios of hardener to resin. The yellow ribbon is the resin, the blue the hardener; I mix them in a ratio of 65% yellow to 35% blue, which makes it less sticky and easier to manipulate on the figure surfaces.

At the time of writing, the author is not aware of any UK-based dealer importing A&B or Duro from the United States. Some British modellers make private arrangements with American friends to supply them with these products in practical amounts - like all epoxy materials, they do have a shelf-life even if carefully stored. Most, however, use the widely available Milliput epoxy putty, which shares most of their essential characteristics. However, miniaturists attempting to use Milliput for the "recipes" given in this book for work with the US products should naturally experiment carefully first, to identify any practical differences in the behaviour of the mediums.

POSING THE FIGURE

Establishing the pose for a figure is by far the most important step in the whole process. If well posed, a figure project gets off on the right track and further detailing and painting only serve to heighten the effect. Conversely, a figure that suffers from disproportionate limbs, a lack of balance or unconvincing body movement can only be camouflaged by a coat of paint. Great care should be taken to ensure that everything is just right at the posing stage before the balance of the sculpting begins.

If the miniaturist is in any doubt about the pose, one obviously useful source of reference can be found in the wide range of instructional books for novice artists. Illustrated guides for beginners in human anatomical drawing often emphasise the proportions of the basic body masses and their

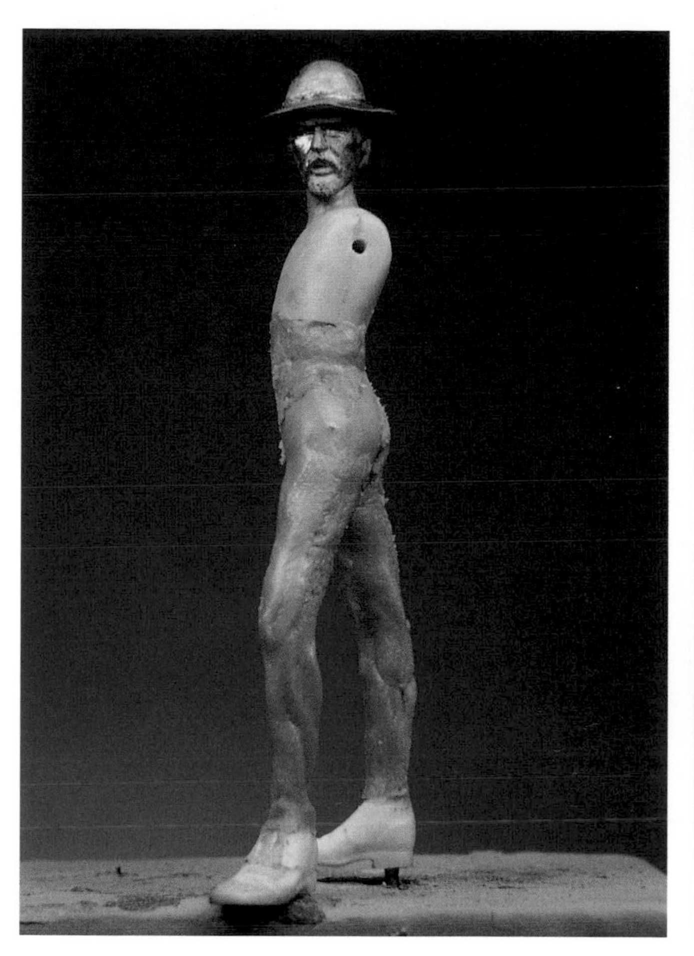

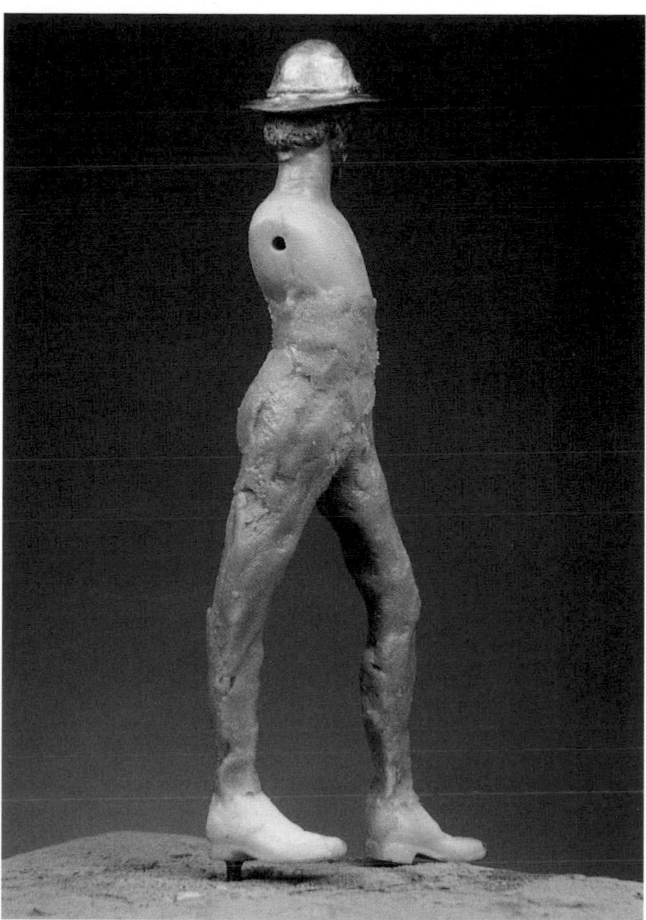

relationships in movement by the use of "block" figures not too dissimilar from the three-dimensional armatures created by miniaturists. A useful three-dimensional reference is the classic articulated wooden "lay figure", also available from art supply shops. (Sadly, the much more complex articulated lay figures of horses are quite rare and usually very expensive.)

The materials used in the initial posing of this figure consisted of three basic components: pre-cast resin upper and lower torsos and shoes, a commercially available head selected for the figure, and a few standard paperclips. Using a low speed motor tool with a drill bit identical in diameter to the paperclip wire, holes were drilled approximately 3/16in. into the mating surfaces of the resin parts to permit attachment of head to upper torso, upper to lower torso, legs (pre-measured wire lengths) to lower torso, arms to shoulders and shoes to legs. The wire used for the legs was deliberately left longer than necessary to allow approximately 1/2in. to protrude from the bottom of the heel, as a pin for attachment to the working and final bases. All attachments were made with superglue.

Once the parts were assembled as described, the fun began. The pose selected for this figure is a casual stance; one would think that such a pose would be easy to achieve - but not necessarily. In order to create a sense of relaxation in the stance the upper torso was tilted slightly backwards and up on the left side, and the head slightly forwards and to the left to provide counterbalance. The right shoulder was given an upwards tilt consistent with the anticipated arm positions, to be added later. The soldier's weight is supported on his right leg, which was given a slight "bow" backwards and to his right - an effect which can be seen by human observation. The left leg is relaxed and slightly bent.

Once the pose was achieved, the neck, waist and legs were covered with a layer of A&B putty, and put in an oven at 140 degrees Fahrenheit for about half an hour to speed up the drying process. It is important to emphasize that this "fleshing out" of the armature parts need not be a particularly artistic undertaking: the entire body will be clothed later in a second layer of putty, completely obscuring this one. As a minimum, the A&B should be applied in such a way that the shape of the body is roughly approximated, and that no voids are left which might trap air and create bubbles in the drying Duro at a later stage.

The next step was the attachment and positioning of the arms and hands. In this case the hands were cut from Airfix Multipose arms at the wrist. All the fingers were cut from the right hand, as this would be holding a pipe, requiring re-articulation of the fingers. The free-hanging left hand was left almost intact, only the thumb being removed - this would be added later from Duro, at a more relaxed angle than the original Airfix part.

A hole was carefully drilled up from the wrist to allow for insertion of the paperclip wire arm. Each wire arm was cut to length and superglued into the holes in the shoulders of the upper torso; they were then manipulated with pliers until the proper angles were achieved. Then the arms in their turn were given a layer of A&B, and set aside to dry.

The pose now being complete, the next phase in the process was the sculpting of the clothing and equipment.

CLOTHING THE FIGURE

As with painting, I prefer to sculpt my figures from the top downwards and "from the inside out". The head used here is a Shenandoah Miniatures accessory, selected for its appropriateness to the subject. Very little alteration was needed, only three minor features being changed from the original casting. New eyes were sculpted to create a squinting facial expression consistent with the summer heat in which the figure was to be depicted. This was done by carefully carving out the existing eyes and adding small football-shaped beads of Duro (for British readers - rugger ball shapes) to each socket. These were grafted into the eye sockets and slit in a downward crescent shape with a sharp toothpick. The sparse chin beard of the casting was lengthened with Duro and textured with the sharp toothpick. Finally, the hat cord on the casting was embellished with two tassels, thus making it a blue infantry hat cord - which would provide a welcome touch of colour on a figure painted mostly in drab tones.

The sculpting of the uniform began with the chest and back. Duro (mixed 65% yellow/35% blue) was spread in a thin, even coat over the chest and back with a toothpick, using a rolling-pin motion; a moistened finger helped hasten the process. The jacket was deliberately made longer than necessary: this allowed the Duro to be sliced off at the proper length once the putty had dried, giving a clean, sharp, unrounded edge. Once the areas had been covered properly, folds were sculpted in with the same toothpick tools. The types of folds appropriate to a figure are largely dictated by the fabric of the uniform; the heavy wool shell jackets worn by Confederate infantrymen create subtle, gentle folds, unlike the more numerous and sharper wrinkles seen in thinner serge or cotton garments. Although the folds are less numerous than they would be on some other figures, those in the armpit area are relatively deeper and more defined due to the stress in this area.

The closure at the front of the jacket was sliced in with a hobby knife, and "opened" with a knifeblade and toothpick. Buttonholes were cut in at intervals, over which buttons were added later. The waist belt was cut from a sheet of copper foil, and gently pressed slightly into the wet Duro, the

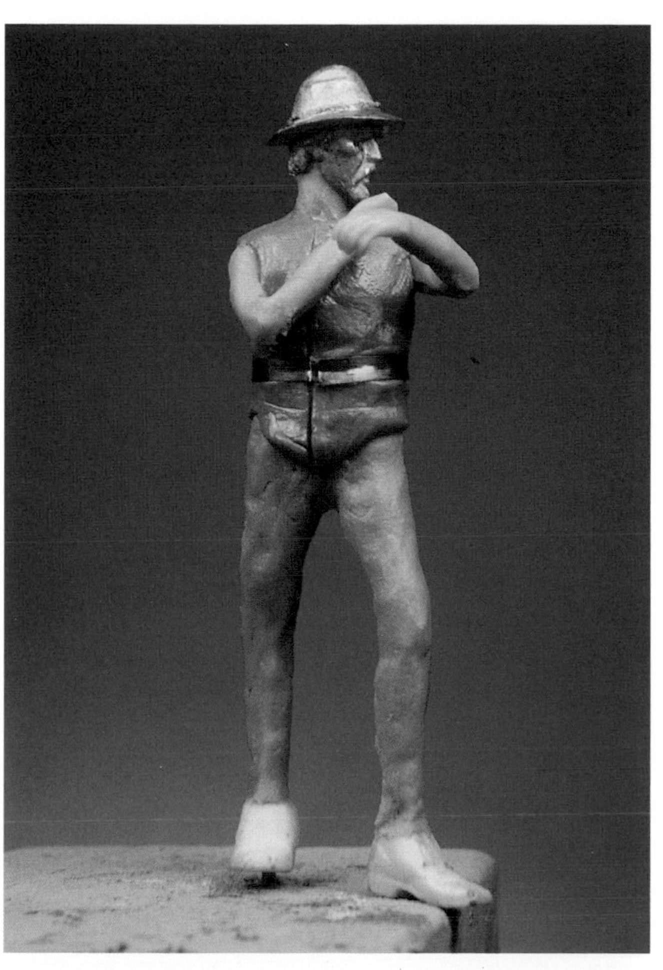

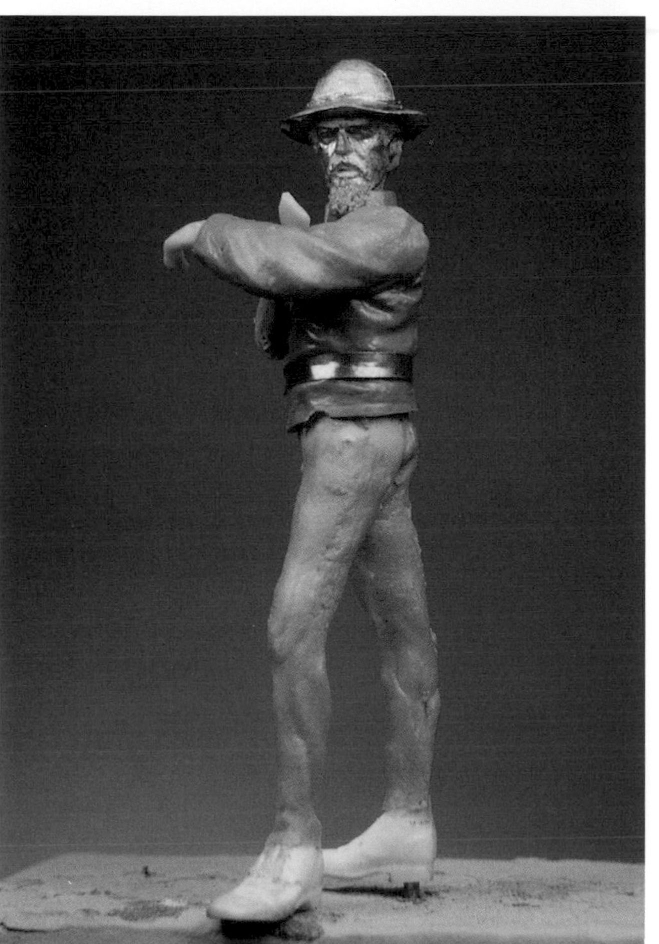

(Far left top & bottom) In order to get the proper elevation for the left arm it was necessary to use the actual rifle - a stock commercial accessory - at this stage. The hands were cut from Airfix Multipose arms, and some of the fingers removed as described in the text. Then the arms in turn were covered with A&B putty; note the shape of the upper arm and shoulder.

(Top right) The first application of Duro clothing to the chest and back, using a toothpick with a "rolling pin" motion; the same tool was later used to form the folds. The bottom of the jacket was left too long at this stage; and a waist belt of sheet copper was countersunk into the Duro.

(Bottom right) Once dry, the jacket was sliced off cleanly. The next step was the left sleeve; the trick here is to portray convincingly its fullness, particularly the roomy elbow characteristic of Confederate jackets. Also added at this stage are the eyes, a fuller beard, and the collar, all from Duro.

jacket folds in this area being modified to accomodate it. The figure was then placed in the oven for 30 minutes at 140F to dry.

The sleeves were tackled next. Confederate shell jackets offer an interesting challenge here due to their - to modern eyes - unusually full sleeves, particularly at the elbow. (It goes without saying that constant reference should be made to authentic pictorial sources when scratch-building or making major conversions.) This was taken into account by applying a thicker layer of putty to the elbow than to the forearm and shoulder areas. Once again, the putty was spread over the arm with a rolling motion, after which folds were sculpted with the toothpick. Constant practice makes the configuring of the folds and wrinkles in a uniform almost second nature; however, it is always a good idea to study the drapery of clothing and make mental notes and sketches, or even to take photographs of drapery effects for future reference. After the left sleeve had been sculpted and allowed to dry the process was repeated on the right sleeve. It is important not to try to sculpt too much in a single "sitting", as the more wet putty there is on a figure at any given moment, the more likely one is to press ones thumb into the middle of a well-sculpted area...I do indeed speak from experience!

The same process was repeated for the trousers, which were also sculpted one at a time. Trouser drapery is more complicated and time-consuming.

(Above) The first step in sculpting the trouser leg, rolling on the putty to the proper thickness; the sock is formed as part of the trousers at this stage.

(Centre photos) The folds and drapery of the trouser legs are added, and the sock delineated; the prominent outer trouser seam is cut into the putty while it is wet. Note the basic shapes of cap pouch and belt buckle also added at this stage, and the tassels added to the hat cord.

The drapery on a simple standing figure is, in fact, more difficult to achieve convincingly than on a very animated figure, as the stress in the clothing is less apparent; this is where careful observation is important. The heavier outer trouser leg seams were carved into the wet putty with a hobby knife; the inner seams - as well as those on the jacket - were only painted. It is worth noting that this soldier has tucked his trousers into his woollen socks; the socks were formed as if they were part of the trousers, socks and trousers being differentiated with a knife during the sculpting process. The shoe tops were sculpted later, as were the laces.

Once the basic garments had been sculpted the focus shifted to the details. At this stage the cap pouch, cartridge box, haversack and strap, fingers, and rolled blanket were added. The same incremental approach taken with the clothing was employed in the sculpting of the equipment and details.

The cap pouch was sculpted in two stages. First, the basic pouch was formed by pressing an appropriately sized blob of Duro to the right of the waist belt, and shaping it correctly with a toothpick, using photographs of the real thing as a guide. The key here was the shape of the pouch, and the definition of the stiff board backing behind it. Once this had dried, the flap was sculpted from a separate piece of Duro; the shape

(Above) The positioning of the haversack and the tin drum canteen; the canteen was gently pressed into the roughly formed haversack to create a sense of weight - this partly determines the final shaping of the folds and wrinkles in the cloth.

of this flap is very distinctive, and careful attention to the reference photographs was vital. The final touch was a tiny ball of Duro for the fastening stud, pressed gently into the flap strap beneath the pouch.

The cartridge box was a resin casting of a part I sculpted some time ago, without the flap: as I intended to use this casting for both open and closed cartridge boxes the flap position needed to be variable. Besides, it is easy to cut a new flap from sheet lead or copper, and the effect is more realistic than a pre-moulded flap. The flap was carefully measured against the box, cut to shape with scissors, and superglued to the box. The assembly was attached with the aid of a small blob of Duro, to ensure that the part "seated" securely against the waist belt.

The haversack and strap were each sculpted from Duro. Obtaining the proper shape for the haversack was the key, and two considerations had to be borne in mind: the objects which were likely to be carried inside the thin cloth bag, and the weight of the drum-shaped tin water canteen resting on it. First the basic shape of the haversack was formed, using a toothpick to block out the shape, and a hobby knife to open out the flap. The edge seams of the linen fabric were defined, and a subtle puckering was applied carefully along the seam edges. The canteen shape - sliced from a hardened, rolled Duro

(Above) Formed from pressed-out A&B putty, the ends of the blanket are rolled up and attached to the figure.

"sausage" - was added while the sculpting was under way. Once the canteen had been pressed into the haversack the remainder of the folds were added to the latter, its thin fabric requiring more widespread and thinner wrinkling than seen on the clothing. A Duro button was the final touch.

The rolled blanket was virtually the last feature added. In order to achieve a realistic end to the blanket roll I decided to use A&B putty flattened to a paper thinness with a rolling pin, then rolled up much as the original blanket might have been.

Flattened A&B comes in very handy for many things, including flowing garments and flags, although great care must be taken in handling it once it has dried - it is VERY brittle. The A&B is allowed to set for about an hour, then pressed flat with fingers coated liberally with Vaseline or talcum powder. The putty is then placed between two sheets of wax paper or cellophane, and rolled as thin as necessary with a rolling pin. Further flattening can be achieved by removing the putty from the cellophane and replacing the rolling pin with a paintbrush handle.

The blanket ends were cut to size and superglued into place on the figure; once in place they were carefully manipulated to the desired position. The balance of the blanket roll was a solid piece of A&B pressed across the figure's body, the transitions to the ends being smoothed by brushing the A&B with a paintbrush moistened with Dio-Sol thinner. The rope ties were made from Duro, rolled vigorously back and forth between the forefinger and a flat surface to form a thin, round "string" to the desired thickness.

The soldier's fingers were also shaped from rolled Duro strings, and grafted onto the hand with a toothpick. Knuckle definition was added once the finger had been securely attached. In the case of this figure the fingers of the right hand and the pipe were added only after most of the figure painting had been completed, to allow easier access for the paintbrush to the face and upper chest. The pipe was made from two different thicknesses of Duro string. The right thumb and forefinger were sculpted first, separated by the approximate size of the pipe; once these had dried the pipe was superglued to these two fingers, and the remaining three fingers were added. The rifle used for this figure is a standard Shenandoah Miniatures accessory, with the sling removed and new sling rings added from Duro.

The sculpting of this figure took approximately 12 hours in all, spread out over five evenings. Good conversion work need not take hundreds of hours if properly planned and systematically undertaken. Of course, the best way to reduce the time necessary to complete a major conversion is simply practice. Repetition breeds efficiency; and the more efficiently one uses one's time, the sooner one can get on to the painting - or the next figure.

(Left top & bottom) The balance of the blanket was sculpted from A&B putty, and smoothed into the already positioned ends with thinners; cords were later added from Duro "string". Note also the cartridge pouch and flap, and cap pouch flap.

(Above) The figure after painting. This enhances the sculpted details such as the ribbing of the socks, the trouser and jacket seams, and subtle wrinkling behind the knee. Please remember that the figure is reproduced here four times actual size.

(Above & right) By comparison, note the more sophisticated basic mannequin created by *John Rosengrant* for his striking 200mm figure of a German Fallschirmjaeger in the Battle of the Bulge, complete with wire finger armatures.

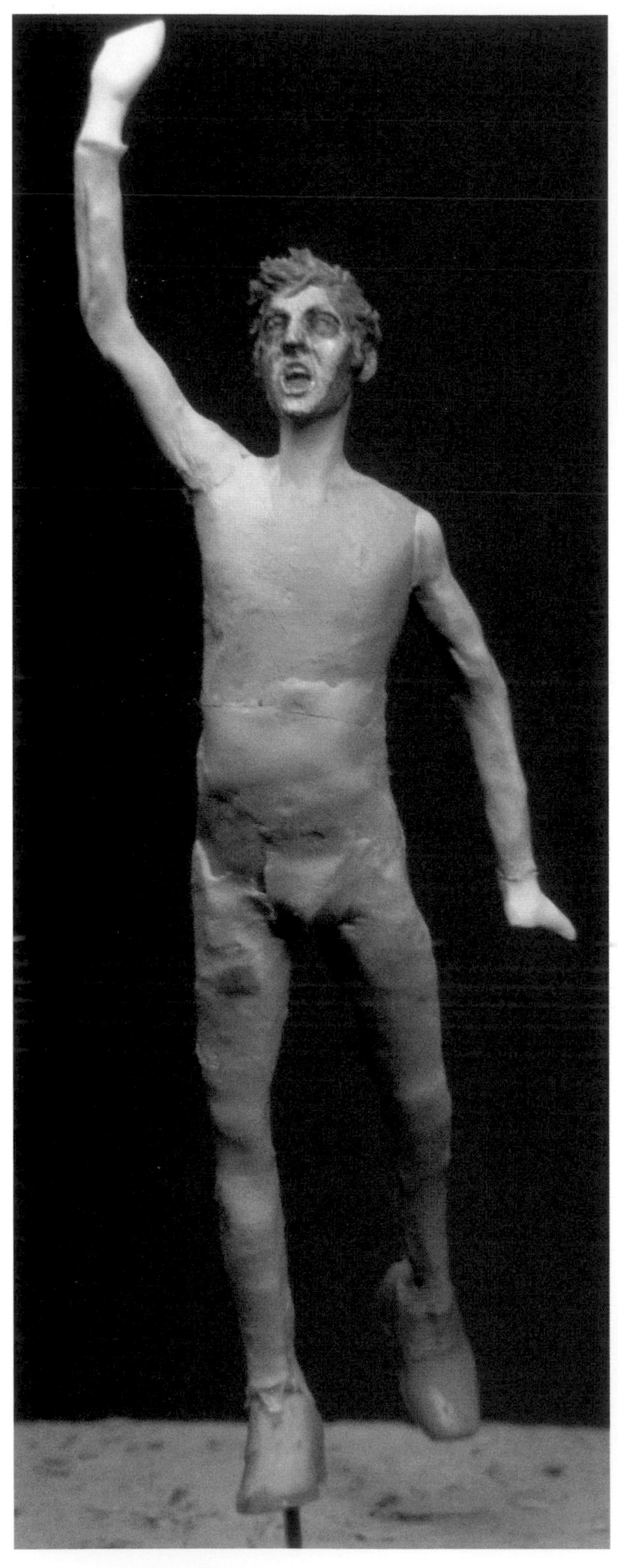

(Above & right) In-process shots of a private of the 24th Foot at Rorke's Drift, 1879, after an Angus McBride painting in Osprey's Men-at-Arms title *The Zulu War*.

The elaborate sporran worn by this officer of the Gordon Highlanders during the 1881 Transvaal War was copied from an example in the Scottish United Services Museum. Unfortunately, I later found from contemporary photos that it was not worn on campaign, and it had to be reworked without all those intricate Duro string details... Note the broadsword hilt in each photo: the shape is formed first, and the steel bars sculpted over it later, the rounded foundation doubling as the liner.

(Above left & right) In-process and painted views of a running private of the 14th Tennessee, 1863. Study of period sources will nearly always suggest small but attractive details - here, the carrying of both rifle and loose ramrod in the hand adds an impression of in-battle urgency.

(Right) The author's first conversion drew heavily on commercially available accessories, at the expense of historical accuracy. I later found out that the wooden canteen carried by this private of the 31st Foot at Sobraon was not used in India.

(Left) This sergeant of the Black Watch at Tamai, 1885, was among the author's first conversions, and serves to remind him that it takes practice to achieve high standards. Compare, e.g., the sporran with that in the photo below.

(Below left) A later attempt at a private of the Black Watch, 1885.

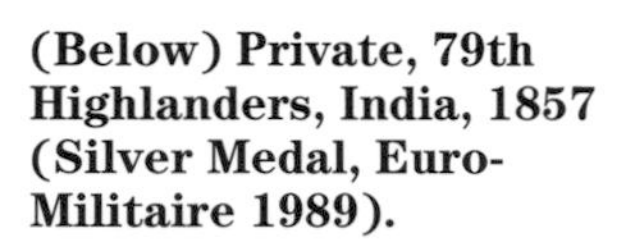

(Below) Private, 79th Highlanders, India, 1857 (Silver Medal, Euro-Militaire 1989).

(Above left) Ensign, 32nd Foot, displaying the Regimental Colour during the storming of Multan in 1848. The colour was made from rolled out A&B putty, with free-hand battle honours and details painted across its folds. Note that highlighting and shading add to the effect of such details as the lettering and scrolls on a colour. ***(Photo:Nick Infield)***

(Left) Sometimes it can be refreshing to take a break from martial poses, as in this depiction of a private of the 78th Highlanders, 1807, offering a rose to a young lady, with an ingratiating leer.

(Above) A quiet scene can speak more eloquently than the flashier battle poses. The face and body-language of this Rifleman of the 95th during the dreadful winter retreat to Corunna convey his exhaustion.

(Right) Colour-sergeant, 93rd Highlanders, 1854. The surviving photographic portraits of the British Regulars in the Crimea include some wonderfully impressive personalities. Their soldierly character, staring proudly out of the page, makes the miniaturist's fingers itch...

(Right) A tribute to a friend and a superb artist, the late Rick Scollins, one of whose black-and-white paintings in the book *British Sieges of the Peninsular War* inspired this sharpshooter of the King's German Legion reloading his Baker rifle amid the ruins. The miniaturist who favours single figures must always be searching for novel presentation ideas, to give his small canvas an immediate identity. Urban debris, which can be striking, tends to get overlooked in pre-20th century subjects, but much fighting has always taken place in and around towns.

(Left) The drum carried by this private of the 2nd Wisconsin Infantry at Gettysburg started life as a Historex part. The mis-shapen cords were carved away and replaced by new ones made from stretched plastic sprue.

(Right & far right) An unusual detail spotted in a museum can bring inspiration - in this case a wooden keg canteen carried by an officer of the Grenadier Guards at the Alma, and now on display in the Guards Museum, London. The canteen was made from a combination of Duro, rolled and sliced to size like a sausage, and sheet plastic/Duro details, with straps from yellow

(Left) Officer, 79th Highlanders, 1854: another opportunity to enjoy painting Cameron of Erracht tartan...

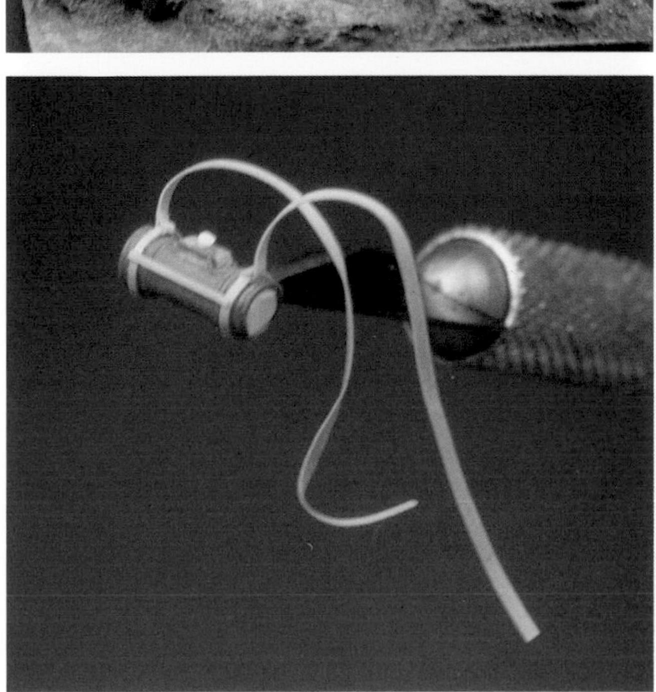

(Left & right) The experienced miniaturist will inevitably sometimes run up against a mental block: he has chosen his subject - but what pose to pick, that he hasn't used before? The answer can sometimes lie in simply checking the research sources for the appropriate series of contemporary weapons-handling drills.

Here, a private of the 22nd (Cheshire) Regiment at Meanee, 1843, gropes in his pouch for another cartridge; a soldier of the 6th (Warwickshires) slips powder and ball into the muzzle of his musket during the 8th Cape Frontier War, 1852; and an Argyll of the 91st Highlanders, fighting on the same frontier in 1846, rams it home.

(Right) By angling this trooper of Custer's 7th Cavalry on a slope, firing in the opposite direction, an impression of stubborn retreat is conveyed. The arrow in the ground at his feet is a silent reminder of the fate awaiting him. (First Place, Paris/Sevres 1991.)

(Left) The same basic trick, of placing the figure on a section of sloping groundwork, justifies an interesting, effortful pose for this officer of the 5th US Cavalry in winter 1885.

(Left) A different problem was presented by this likeness of Brigadier General Joseph B.Davis, 1863. To portray the diminutive nephew of the Confederate President Jefferson Davis, a smaller body was married to a standard 54mm head to create an impression of small stature.

(Below) Brigadier General John Buford commanded the Federal cavalry division that first engaged the Confederates at the outset of the Battle of Gettysburg. For obvious reasons, the post and rail fence had to be constructed before the figure could be posed. This miniature is an interesting example of how even a glaring impossibility, like this cut-off fence disappearing into space, can be pulled off without offending the eye of the viewer so long as it is carefully planned.

(Above left) Private, Princess Charlotte of Wales's Berkshire Regiment (the old 49th) at the Battle of Ginniss, 1886 - one of the last campaigns fought wearing the red coat. The miniaturist will really appreciate top-quality brushes when painting "BERKSHIRE" across a 54mm scale shoulder strap. (Gold Medal, Euro-Militaire 1989.)

(Left) Some miniaturists set their face against models depicting campaign wear-and-tear, and it can certainly be overdone if attempted without sensitive restraint. But the fact remains that a severe toll was taken on parade ground uniforms by, say, the 19th century South African bush. Note the dirty, worn look of this 1846 Rifleman's clothing, and the locally made sandals replacing worn-out boots - features confirmed by eye-witness accounts.

(Above) A private of the 92nd Highlanders at Lucknow, 1857: again, note the value of elevation in presenting the figure, the steepness of the slope giving an impression of quite a drop below. The opening up of the gaiter and hose reminds us of one of the most important goals of the miniaturist: to fashion what is essentially a solid object in such a way as to give an impression of several thin, overlayed layers of clothing.

(Above) Ideas for posing military miniatures can come from almost anywhere, and the eye should constantly be alert. This officer of the 42nd Highlanders at the Alma, 1854, was inspired by watching family members bowling on a Sunday afternoon.

(Above right) Private, 51st Light Infantry, 1812; here the pose and groundwork combine to create the effect of a charging soldier coming up over a crest.

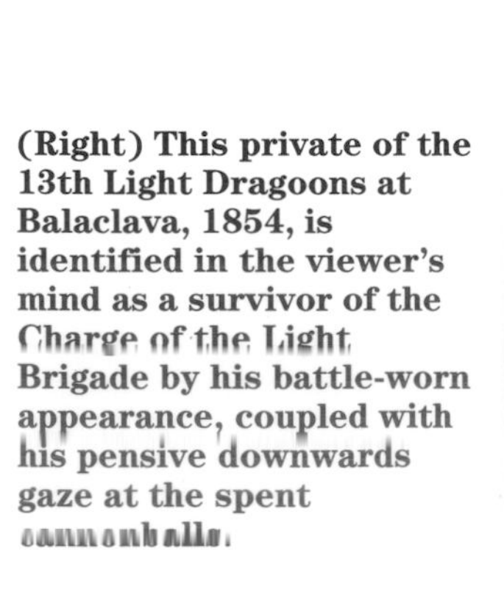

(Right) This private of the 13th Light Dragoons at Balaclava, 1854, is identified in the viewer's mind as a survivor of the Charge of the Light Brigade by his battle-worn appearance, coupled with his pensive downwards gaze at the spent cannonballs.

(Above left & right) This trooper of the 6th Dragoon Guards in India, 1857, was based on an illustration by Pierre Turner in Osprey's Men-at-Arms title *The British Army on Campaign 1816-1902 (3)*.

(Left) Private, Highland Light Infantry, 1859.

(Above left) Officer, 46th Georgia Infantry, 1864. Time spent on such details as the right wrist area here is never wasted.

(Left) It may seem obvious to mention it, but the facial expression should match the pose of the body. This private of the 14th Brooklyn, 1862, is clearly running towards something, not away from something.

(Above) Private, 11th Mississippi Infantry, Gettysburg, 1863. Note the broken laces on the brogan; and also the highlighting and shading of the lettering painted on the battle flag.

(Above left) Private, Gordon Highlanders, 1908, based on an Angus McBride illustration in Osprey's Men-at-Arms *North-West Frontier 1837-1947.*

(Above) Another of the author's earlier conversions, depicting a colour-sergeant of the Grenadier Guards in the Crimea. In this case an otherwise interesting figure was somewhat marred by the inaccurate knapsack and greatcoat, which further research revealed were replaced by a blanket roll in the early stages of the 1854 campaign.

(Left) A Hottentot irregular of the Cape Frontier Wars.

(Above) Part of the charm of obscure subjects lies in their unexpected appearance as soldiers on campaign. Clad in a Norfolk-cut tunic and corduroys, this officer of the 6th Foot in the Cape, 1851, looks more like a gentleman on a weekend hunting trip.

(Above right) Confederate infantryman, 1865. Without any significant differences in uniform during the Civil War, the miniaturist can still achieve a sense of period by visually emphasising the privations suffered by the Confederates in the final stages - hence the bare feet. The wildflowers make an attractive addition to groundwork.

(Right) Based on an Angus McBride illustration from Osprey's Men-at-Arms *Napoleon's Guard Cavalry*, this trumpeter of German Light Horse seems to be daring anyone to make snide comments about his pink jacket...

(Above left) Rapid movement is best portrayed by placing a figure in an off-balance posture, like this officer of the 140th New York Infantry, 1864, who is pinned to the base through the toe of his right shoe.

(Above) A private of the 79th Highlanders leaping into the Russian positions at the Alma, 1854, offers another example of extreme movement. For poses like this it is important to check carefully how almost every individual part of the costume and equipment would behave during a specific body motion.

(Left) Painting white linen uniforms is an interesting challenge, as the wrinkling is far tighter and more intricate than the folds which form in heavier fabrics. On this model of an officer of US Marines, 1859, note particularly the armpit and waist areas.

(Above) Officer, Cameron Highlanders, Tel el Kebir, 1882 - based on a painting by the superb French battle artist Alphonse De Neuville. Conviction is added to miniatures by converting stock heads to produce individual portraits with features, hairstyles and other details matching the "look" of a specific period and nationality.

(Above right) The posing of this officer of the York and Lancaster Regiment, fighting in the Sudan in 1885, directs the viewer's eye in such a way as to create an impression of a real but unseen world "off stage".

(Right) The ornate mitre cap of the 18th century grenadier offers a demanding challenge in detail painting, as does the many-layered and lavishly laced uniform of the period. Private, Barrell's Regiment, Culloden, 1746.

(Above) Unhorsed but defiant in the Russian snows, an 1812 French Cuirassier crafted by Canadian master *Peter Twist.* Peter makes use of Poste Militaire spare parts to supplement his scratch-building. Metal surfaces such as the cuirass and sword blade are cast in metal and burnished to a bright finish for added realism.

(Right) This dramatically posed "Achilles", a large scale scratch-built figure by *Peter Karel,* won a gold medal at the 1993 Chicago Show.

(Above) *Andrei Koribanics* dazzled spectators at the 1993 World Expo in Washington with this superb First World War German trench raider. The sculpting of the figure, the painting, groundwork and staging all combine in a truly memorable piece of modelling.

(Above right) One of Britain's most daring miniaturists, *Steve Warrilow* is not afraid to take chances with figure poses. This Highland clansman, cornered in a narrow gully, is among his best.

(Right) Historical portrait likenesses are a pleasant diversion. Here *Joe Berton* - perhaps best known for his several striking models of Lawrence of Arabia - depicts Admiral Lord Nelson.

(Above left) ***Mike Good*** **brings an obscure, colourful Eastern Mediterranean subject to life with his model of a member of Wurmer's Frei Corps.**

(Above) As these in-progress shots show, ***Mike Good*** **makes use of a variety of maerials in his converted and scratch-built figures, including Duro, A&B, Milliput, Plumber's Seal, and sheet plastic.**

(Left) Private, 155th Pennsylvania Infantry, 1864. Based on a painting by the renowned artist Don Troiani, this figure was sculpted from A&B putty by ***Dave Peschke.***

(Above left) Highland Clansman, 1745 - a gold medal winner for the author at the 1988 Euro-Militaire competition.

(Above) Officer, 9th US Cavalry, 1885, by *Mike Good* - after Frederick Remington.

(Right) An excellent example of a simple conversion of a commercial kit, painted and presented very effectively! *Jim Johnston* entitled this one "Sharpshooter's Prize".

CHAPTER 3

VIGNETTES

"Vignette" is rather a vague term, interpreted within the context of military miniatures as a small scene including a limited number of figures. Most miniaturists equate the term vignette with a scene of limited size - that is, the size of the base on which the figures are placed; and vignettes tend to be mounted on bases two to five inches across, either square, rectangular or circular. One major European competition defines the term vignette as meaning a scene containing only two or three figures.

All of this is somewhat academic; whatever the physical mechanics, the essential nature of a vignette is that it is a small "three-dimensional story" involving more than one character.

By far the most critical element in any vignette is the selection of a strong central focus. In simpler two-figure vignettes the interaction between the figures is the only focus, and often little else need be added. In scenes involving more than two figures, the viewer's eyes should be drawn to a key feature as defined by the miniaturist; other elements of the vignette, including other figures, should support and direct attention to the central focus. The central focus could be a key figure - such as a standard bearer, say, or an officer - or a pair of figures engaged in a compelling action. The miniaturist must carefully plan the focal point of the vignette, including the manner in which the central importance of that focal point will be conveyed to the viewer.

Obviously, before the planning can begin, the miniaturist must select a subject. I find that reading first-hand accounts of historical events, and good narrative histories focusing on single battles or individuals, are ideal sources of inspiration. Such books are often filled with potential vignettes, as are such publications as *Tradition*, *Military History*, *Military Illustrated*, *Great Battles* and *Gettysburg Magazine*.

It was an article in *Gettysburg Magazine* that inspired a recent vignette entitled **"The Fight for the Flag".** The article described a fascinating confrontation that took place on the first day of that legendary battle: a single Federal regiment spearheaded an attack which crushed an entire Confederate brigade, suffering heavy casualties in the process, and after a brief but furious confrontation captured a Rebel regimental colour. The Federal regiment was the 6th Wisconsin, part of the famous Iron Brigade, and the flag they captured was that of the 2nd Mississippi from Brigadier General Joseph B.Davis' Brigade. The furious struggle for the flag was what caught my interest, and descriptions of the fight from participants in the opposing regiments provided marvellous detail for the vignette.

***"The Fight for the Flag":* close-up of the central focus of the completed vignette.**

PLANNING THE SCENE

The decision to make the struggle for the flag between a Federal corporal and the Confederate colour bearer the central focus of the vignette was fairly obvious, given the nature of the incident portrayed. The next element to be resolved was the "supporting cast". As several soldiers were wounded or killed during the struggle around the flag, their inclusion helped not only to frame the scene, but also to bring home the bloody cost of the conflict. The positioning and posing of these figures had to be achieved in such a way that they supplemented the central struggle for the flag and directed attention towards it, rather than distracting from it by diffusing the focus.

Using the techniques described in Chapter Two, all six figures were wired together in mannequin form to enable them to be posed as a group on the actual base to be used. While standard cast resin upper/lower torsos and shoes were used, the selection of the heads was critical. Shenandoah Miniatures had recently come out with a set of six superb 54mm heads, several of which featured shouting and grimacing facial expressions ideally suited for several of the figures in the scene. As the Shenandoah heads were a bit larger than those commercially available from such manufacturers as Hornet and Verlinden, it was found that only Puchala offered an assortment of heads compatible in size. (Similarly, the larger head size required the figure proportions to be somewhat larger as well - similar in size to Historex figures, for which both Shenandoah and

Puchala heads are well suited.) Pre-cast hair was carved away - I prefer to either sculpt my own hair, or have a "hairless" head on which to sculpt a hat or cap; and the heads were pinned to the upper torso.

After hours of manipulating these miniature "Action Men", I was finally satisfied that the composition was tight and the interaction between the two main characters was suitably dynamic. Among the supporting cast, the wounded lieutenant to the left of the scene points his pistol at the Confederate officer behind the central figures, the angle of arm and pistol almost literally pointing the viewer to the centre of the scene. The Confederate officer looks toward the Federal corporal, the angle of his sword once again pointing towards the centre. The wounded Federal private to the right has his back turned to the viewer, his grimacing face visible only from the back of the vignette. However, even in this posture his presence makes a contribution - the angle of his back and knapsack once again creating a strong diagonal slope towards the centre. Finally, the dead Confederate private in the foreground provides a foundation to the scene, and foreshadows the fate of several figures within the scene.

Typically, I don't advocate the use of round bases for figures and dioramas. Most compelling figures, vignettes and dioramas have a clear front, back and sides, and one will notice that most viewers (and judges!) show little interest in the back of a scene, meaning that extra touches visible only from the back frequently go unappreciated. Of course, this is not to say the back of a scene should not be sculpted, painted and detailed as carefully as the front; but time-consuming added features are usually shown off to best advantage when they can be viewed from the front of a scene.

However, in this case, the angles of the figures comprising the scene opened up some interesting elements which would not be visible from the front, such as the mortally wounded Federal private and the sword-wielding Confederate officer. Even the Federal lieutenant was more clearly visible from behind. Additionally, I decided to add a bit of debris to the patch of open ground behind the Confederate officer and this, coupled with the added interest of the alternative figure-viewing angles, made the choice of a round base seem not just desirable but necessary.

CONVERTING THE FIGURES

Once the figures had been posed and the composition determined, each figure was sculpted, detailed and painted. Many miniaturists prefer to sculpt all the figures in a vignette or diorama before they paint any of them. I prefer to alternate my painting and sculpting; if I go for too long without painting a figure I tend to get out of practice and become inefficient. Besides, once a figure has been sculpted I simply can't wait to see it painted.

The techniques used in creating these figures were virtually identical to those described in Chapter Two. However, a variety of particular challenges arose during the conversion process, and it is upon these areas that I will focus in this section.

(Far left) The posing of all the figures on the base was crucial if a tight, compelling composition was to be achieved. Here, the "action men" are placed in relative position to one another. Note the minimal dead space left around the figures; in addition to other benefits, this makes a visual implication that the scene is only a part of a larger action taking place outside the boundaries of the base.

(Centre) The central focus of the scene is the struggle for the flag. Note the forward lunging position of the Confederate (right), and the backward "pull" of the Federal corporal. Shoulder angles must support the planned arm movements of the figures.

(Right) The sculpting of the Federal corporal in its early stages. Note the flattened A&B hat brim, and the sheet plastic crown supported at the proper elevation by a blob of Duro.

Confederate lieutenant:

The head for this figure was taken from the old Monarch War Elephant Crew, sculpted by Roger Saunders. Unfortunately the ears were in poor condition and required replacement, which was done with Duro. The right arm of this figure being raised in an almost vertical position significantly influenced the positioning of the armature, particularly the rib cage, which was tilted upward on the figure's right side. To accentuate the movement the right leg was also lifted, with only the tip of the right boot touching the ground. The beard had to be added out of the normal sequence, as its length required it to be sculpted to the upper front of the frock coat. The top of the kepi was made from sheet plastic, with the remainder of the cap, except for the electrical tape chin strap, made from Duro.

The two contenders for the flag:

These figures had to be posed together to ensure the proper angles for the arms and legs. The knees of the two figures were in contact with one another. Once the posing had been completed, the figures were sculpted one at a time, care being taken to ensure that the fit of the figures was not affected by the addition of any of the details. Flattened A&B putty was used for the brim of the corporal's hat and the skirts of his uniform coat, and for the Confederate's blanket roll. The Federal's socks were sculpted as a continuation of each trouser leg, *prior* to the detailing of the tops of the brogans (shoes). Cast resin was used for the Federal soldier's blanket roll and for the cartridge boxes, the latter with sheet lead flaps. Both heads were Shenandoah Miniatures accessories.

Federal lieutenant:

The sculpting of this figure was very similar to that of the Federal corporal with a few minor exceptions. The entire hat was done in A&B putty beneath a sheet plastic crown, with hat ornaments detailed in Duro. I experimented with rolled-out Duro for the skirts, as some of this putty was available ready mixed at the time and I preferred not to waste it. It was more difficult to form than the A&B, and the experiment, although successful here, was not repeated.

The right sleeve of the jacket was sculpted from A&B; the stress to the fabric created by the left hand grasping the wounded shoulder required more fluidity to the sleeve than could be achieved with the stiffer Duro. First the left hand and fingers were sculpted to the right shoulder. Next the A&B was applied and roughly formed with a toothpick, and the draping brushed into the putty using Dio-Sol as a medium.

The filter water bottle was shaped by rolling a piece of Duro back and forth on a counter top until a sausage-like shape was achieved. This "sausage" was then gently pressed on a smooth block of wood until the proper kidney-shaped top view was achieved, after which the putty was allowed to dry. The dried shape was sliced to the proper height with an X-Acto knife, after which Duro fittings and an electrical tape strap were attached.

(Above) Sculpting proceeded in stages. Here the right leg and sock have been formed, as have the hat and the first layer of the knapsack.

(Above right) Sculpting is virtually complete, and the corporal is ready for priming. The various materials and putties used are visible in this photograph. Note the open collar, cuffs and pouches.

(Right) The view from the figure's left side shows the detailing of the haversack, and the heavy outer seam on the trousers, cut in with an X-Acto knife while the putty was still wet. Note the angle of the left foot, important for this stance.

Federal private:
The "gut-shot" private was sculpted in virtually identical sequence to that of the corporal, minus the hat. The trick was the positioning of this figure on the base. The location of the various knees and feet of the figures in the vignette dictated the posing of this figure to a great extent. Once again a Shenandoah Miniatures head was used, this time one with an appropriately agonised grimace.

Dead Confederate:
Like the wounded Federal, the body of the dead Confederate was positioned so as to avoid the feet of other figures in the vignette, particularly the central couple struggling for the flag. In order to get a natural fit to the terrain, it was necessary to form the groundwork on which this figure would be positioned before sculpting began; the figure was repeatedly matched up to

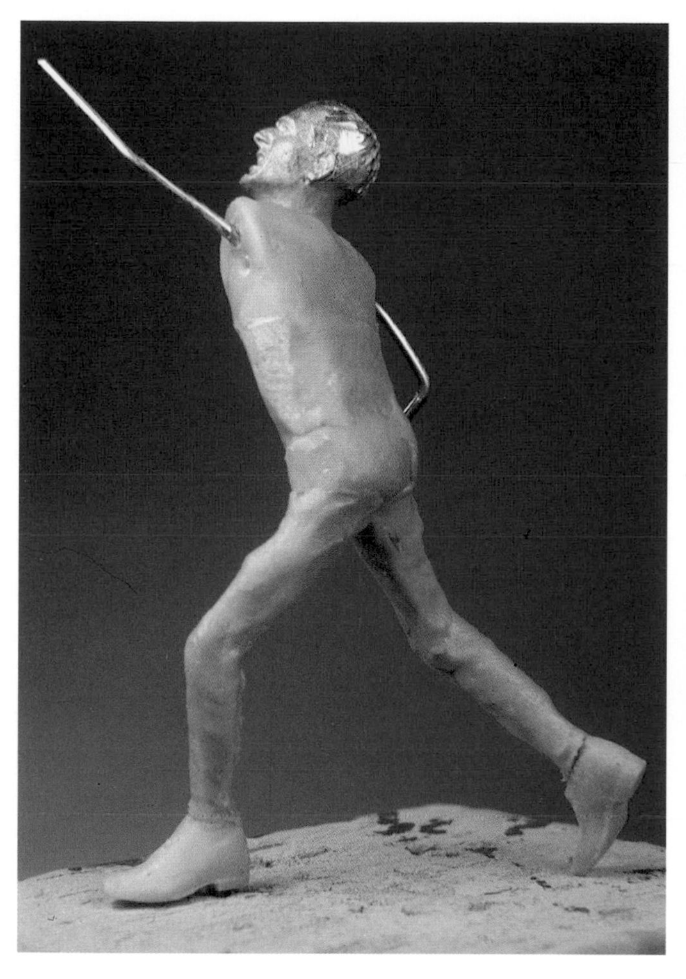

(Above left & right) The lunging pose of the Confederate is further accentuated by the arm position. The angle of the head, established earlier, is an important element in this pose - his eyes are fixed on the flag for which he is fighting. The figure was sculpted almost entirely from Duro, with the exception of the flattened and rolled A&B blanket.

the groundwork during the process of sculpting to ensure that he would fit properly. The bare feet were carved from Airfix Multi-Pose boots (a surprisingly easy task, as it turned out). The hat was made in two parts. First the brim was formed from flattened A&B putty, an oval hole being cut in the center while the putty was stiff but not yet dry; a separate A&B crown was added after the balance of the hat had dried. Joints were smoothed out with a fresh, brushed-out coat of A&B, and Duro was used for the sweat band.

The flag:

The flag proved to be the biggest challenge in the scene. Because it was being grasped and pulled from one end by the Confederate corporal, tension had to be visible in the flag itself. Unfortunately, Confederate flags were tied to their staves with cords; and keeping the wet putty adhering to the top of the flag staff *and* the Confederate corporal's hand was very difficult indeed. The proper shape was finally achieved on the third try. Once the flag had dried, additional wrinkles and stretching were brushed on to it with A&B. The flag staff is wooden dowel, purchased in a doll's house shop, and the flag strings are Duro.

PAINTING THE FIGURES

Before painting the figures in a vignette or diorama it is important to determine the condition of the soldiers' kit. Was the weather dry and dusty? Had it rained that morning, turning the roads into mud? Did the soldiers have a long march to the battle, or were they in camp nearby prior to the episode depicted in the vignette? Was the soil a pale dust colour or red clay? What was the climate - hot and humid, or cool and dry? These are all important questions to which answers should be found before the figures are painted.

In dry summer weather armies on the march generated enormous dust clouds, which not only caked the soldiers' shoes and trouser legs but the rest of their clothing and equipment as well. It is well documented that 1 July 1863 was a very hot, humid day, with temperatures in the 80F range and humidity at a similar level. The Confederate brigade had a somewhat shorter march to Gettysburg that day than the Iron Brigade, but the appearance of the soldiers of both armies must have been less than "parade ground".

To capture the dusty appearance of the soldiers, Humbrol Flesh and Natural Wood colours were mixed into the blues and grays of the uniforms while they were still wet, creating a clear discoloration of the garments. Particularly heavy weathering was applied to the boots, lower trousers and knees; however, earth colours were

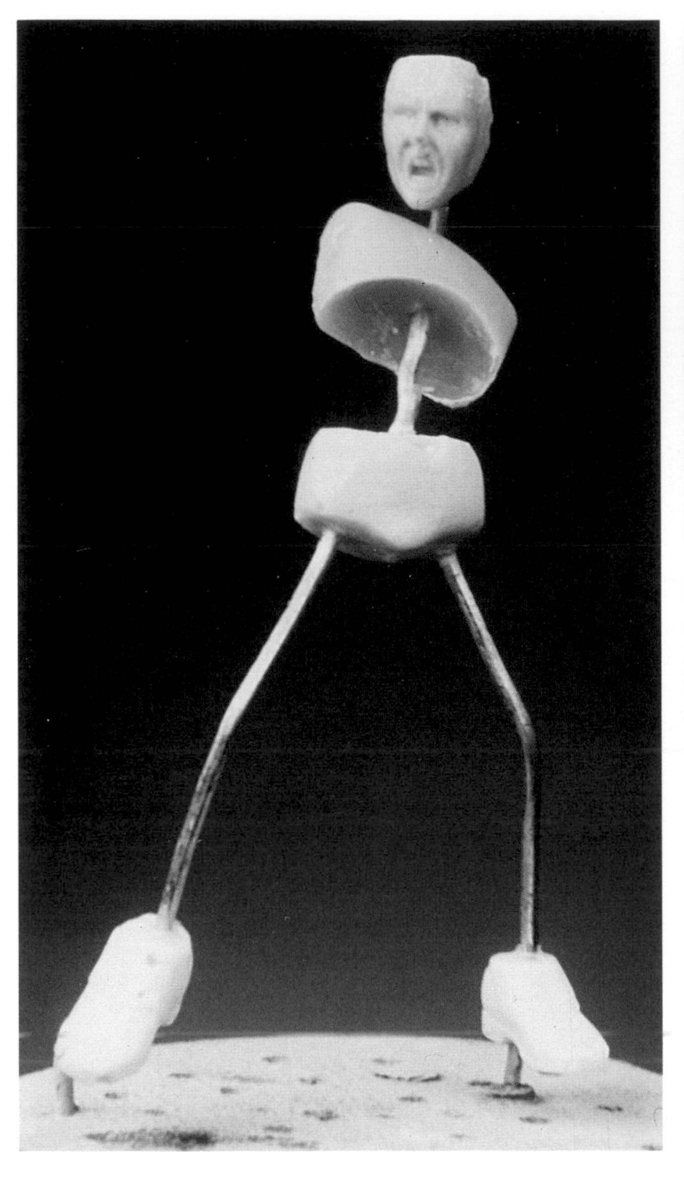

mixed into the wet base colours in varying degrees on numerous portions of the clothing. During the shading of the uniforms, shadow and highlight colours were adjusted to make them more compatible with the varying shades of weathered clothing. This made the shading somewhat more time-consuming, but the end result justified the effort.

The most challenging aspect of the painting of this vignette was the detailing of the figures. Using the plentiful reference material available for Civil War uniforms and equipment, such details at jacket and trouser seams, embroidery on the Federal officer's hat insignia and haversack, Confederate sleeve and kepi details, corporals' stripes, and the embossed letters on belt and cartridge box plates were done with a 000 brush, care being taken to keep the paint consistency perfectly balanced to assure razor-thin, accurate detailing. The exposed shoe soles of the Federal officer and private offered the opportunity to add the sole stitching ... and a hole being worn through the shoe of the Federal private.

The detailing on the Confederate flag was copied from a photograph of the actual flag, and painted freehand. The major features of the flag were painted and shaded first, including the red field and blue/white bars. After these had dried, the stars and battle honours were added. Centring battle honours on flags can be tricky; however, the task can be made relatively simpler by painting the "middle" letter of each in the centre of the space in which the word is to be printed. For example, "Malvern Hill" has 12 letters (counting the space between words as a letter), so the visual centre is the notional line between "r" and "n" . Once this central element is painted the rest of the letters are painted outward in either direction. Of course, it is still crucial that the letters be spaced carefully to prevent them from "bunching up", or unnatural gaps from being left on either side. A little practice in this type of painting can work wonders. Once the basic letters were painted the top edges were highlighted with thin, carefully applied lines. This extra step helps to make the printing jump out at the viewer and adds a three-dimensional look to the flag.

THE GROUNDWORK AND FINAL DETAILS

The groundwork for this vignette was also made from A&D putty in similar fashion to that for the Highlander described in Chapter One, and the soil colour was mixed and applied using the same techniques. The tall grass is

(Far left) Extremes of movement are exciting. This Confederate officer is not just trying to strike the Federal corporal, he seems determined to slice him in two... Note the angles of the torso, head and legs.

(Centre) The sculpting of the Confederate officer is approximately 20% complete at this stage. Note the Duro ears, and the construction of the kepi, similar to that used for the Federal corporal's hat.

(Left) The Confederate officer required a more liberal use of A&B than most figures, due to the length of the skirts and the fuller, flowing frock coat sleeves. The sword blade was a Historex accessory, scraped down to less than half its original thickness.

(Below left) The Federal lieutenant, ready for priming; note the pin supporting his knee at the correct height.

(Below) The Federal lieutenant completed and painted, rear view. Note the detail painting of the oval hat patch, a black velvet background with a gold Union eagle grasping arrows and oak leaves, edged in gold. Note also the stitching on the soles of the boots, the haversack detail, the painted identification on the filter water bottle, and the hardtack crackers on the ground.

unravelled jute twine, painted Humbrol Grass Green, cut to size and applied to white glue with dog-legged tweezers. The tiny flowers duplicated those actually seen in the summer months on this part of the battlefield, and are plucked from dried flowers purchased in a craft shop. After carefully gluing them to the grassy areas of the groundwork they were painted yellow.

An important element in the depiction of any battle is the presence of debris. Most soldiers discard items of equipment to make marching, manoeuvre or flight easier - and many accounts mention that soldiers of the War Between the States were particularly prone to lightening their loads. Damaged items were simply tossed on the ground, hats fell off, and wounded men dropped their rifles. I added a number of items to the open sections of the groundwork, including two rifles, Federal and Confederate hats, a handful of Minie cartridges, and a few pieces of "hardtack" - the dimpled crackers issued to Federal troops. These were made by flattening a piece of Duro and carefully poking four rows of holes, four holes per row, into the wet putty; once it had dried the square shape was sliced around the dimples. Painting was accomplished after gluing the hardtack to the ground.

One might think that a base 3 1/2 inches in diameter would be too small to hold a six-figure vignette; but the tightness of the composition, and the interaction of the figures combined to make the scene dynamic, with no wasted space. A clear idea of the focal point in the scene, a supporting cast that compliments and supports that focus, and an absolute minimum of unnecessary dead space are the keys to success in vignette composition.

(Below) Front and rear views of the completed and painted mortally wounded Federal private.

The completed *"Fight for the Flag"* seen from two different angles. Its effect when viewed from all directions had to be considered from the earliest planning stage. The decision to make an "all-round" vignette involves a conscious sacrifice of the miniaturist's control over the viewer's angle of vision, and all the practical implications should be thought through carefully.

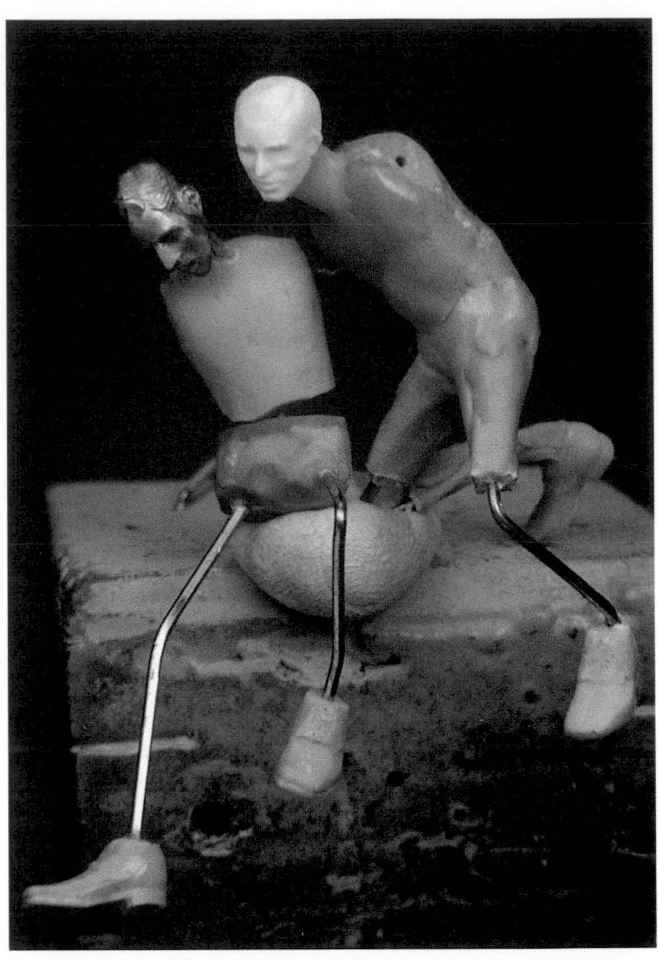

(Above) *"Incident in the Waterkloof"*, a vignette portraying 74th Highlanders and 6th Foot in an encounter battle in close country on the Cape Frontier, South Africa, in 1851. The author makes no apology for his enthusiasm for this subject, given the dramatic settings, and the attractive campaign modifications to British Army uniforms recorded in these wars. Note how the firing redcoat in the background indicates the proximity of danger, and the shouting Highlander in the foreground pulls in the attention of the viewer as he calls for help.

(Above right) The initial posing for the central focus of the vignette. Note the tilt of the heads, and the angles of the torsos and hips. The officer at left has been fitted with a Scale Link head, while that of the private at right is an Airfix Multipose spare.

(Opposite top left) The arms were posed, and the entire armature solidified with A&B putty. The initial posing completed, the sculpting begins with the reworking of the eyes and addition of the private's headgear.

(Above) The completed central figures after painting, as seen within the context of the vignette.

(Left) Two photos showing the sculpting complete. Note the built-up noses, the officer's in A&B and the private's in Duro. The white areas were built up and smoothed over with white A&B putty, a finer grained alternative to the tan variety.

(Top left) Private of the 6th Foot after sculpting; and painted and set into the vignette. Note the fine wrinkling across the lap of the cotton trousers.

(Bottom left) The shouting private of the 74th Highlanders ready for priming - note the Verlinden left hand; and painted and set into his position in the foreground of the vignette.

(Above) The officer's Hottentot bearer wears a hat with a sloping brim made from sheet lead, and hands taken from the Verlinden spares box. Once again, note the tight wrinkling in the thin fabrics of his clothing.

(Right) The groundwork for *"Incident in the Waterkloof"* vignette prior to figure attachment. Note the liberal use of dried flowers from a craft shop, roots, static and longer jute twine grass.

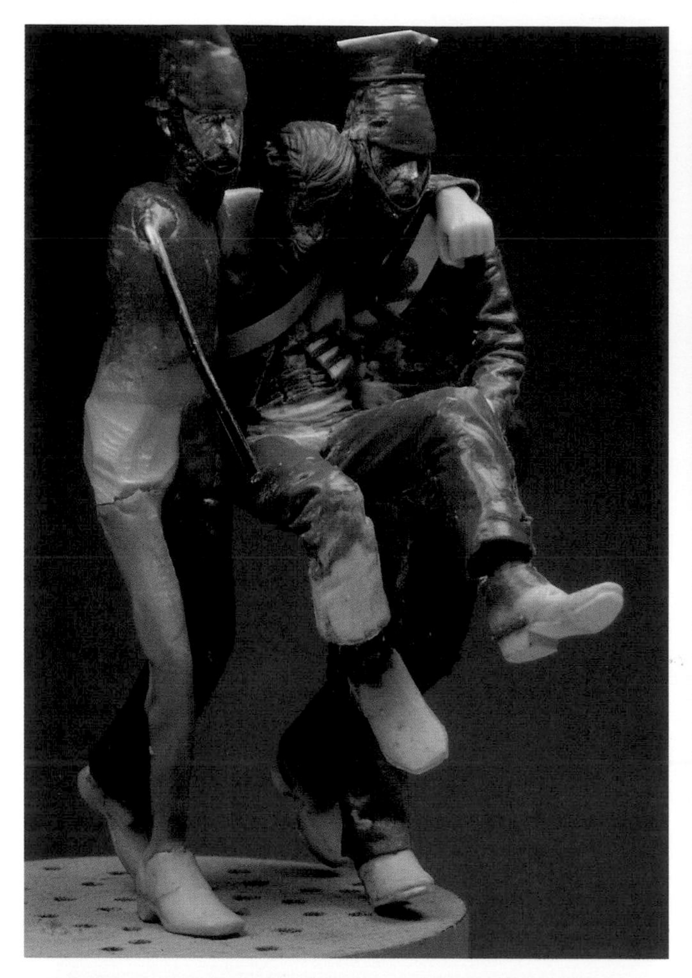

(Above left) ***"Casualty of War":*** **Balaclava, 25 October 1854 - two 17th Lancers carry a wounded 11th Hussar from the field. Correctly sculpting this type of interaction between three different moving figures is extremely difficult, and careful observation and planning are essential. Note the inwards-turned upper bodies of the men carrying the wounded hussar, and his raised shoulders. Liberal amounts of white A&B putty were used to build up transitional areas. Note also the sheet plastic crowns on the lance caps.**

(Left) ***"Casualty of War"*** **completed and painted.**

(Above) Rear view in-process shot; note the arms sculpted virtually as parts of the other figures.

(Right) ***"Stand Fast, You Boys From Maine!"*** **depicts Colonel Joshua Lawrence Chamberlain and the 20th Maine at Little Round Top during the second day of the Battle of Gettysburg - a subject made famous by Michael Shaara's Pulitzer Prize winning novel** ***The Killer Angels.*** **Note how the boulders provide a convenient means of varying the levels of the figures.**

(Above) Detail of the scene, showing a lieutenant drawing his sword.

(Above right) A wounded Confederate lies at the foot of the boulders. Note the horizontal stratifications in the boulders, which were cut from styrofoam, coated in A&B and textured while the putty was wet. The fallen tree is a root with smaller roots glued into pre-drilled holes in the trunk; the entire tree was carefully painted in enamels. The green leaves are photo-etched brass, fallen leaves are crumbled parsley flakes.

(Right) The Union standard bearer. The colour was flattened A&B putty painted in enamels; the gold stars were painted in yellow ochre tones, shaded with burnt umber washes and highlighted with thin whitish yellow lines along the top edges to create a "stitched-on" appearance.

(Left) Detail showing a wounded Maine private drawing his bayonet.

(Below left) Close-up of the Federal lieutenant. Note the blackish powder stains on his cheeks, the puckering along the lower seam of his sack coat, and the tilt of his hat.

(Below) A close-up of Chamberlain and the central tableau. Note the eagle and wreath detailing on Chamberlain's belt plate, and the red Maltese cross badge of 1st Division, V Corps.

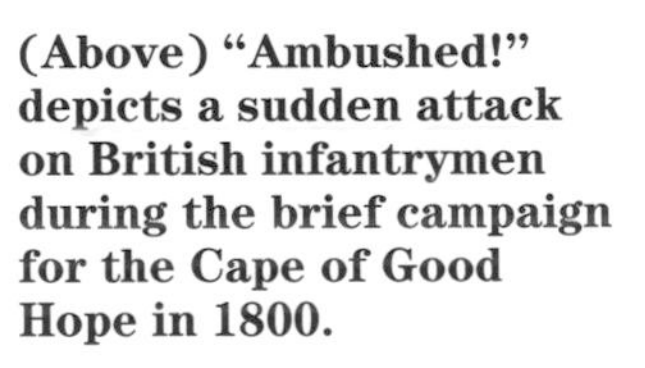

(Above) "Ambushed!" depicts a sudden attack on British infantrymen during the brief campaign for the Cape of Good Hope in 1800.

(Above right) In "Albuhera", three desperate British soldiers are surrounded by implied French cavalrymen just beyond the imaginary plane of the base.

(Right) "The Last Request: Spion Kop, 1899". The exact tilt of the right-hand soldier's head was important, to create a listening effect.

(Below) Another good example of the use of varying levels in a vignette is "General Gough at Mudki". The presence of the horse and the figure on the forward slope are central to the effect. General Gough's unique white "fighting coat", now on display in the National Army Museum in London, helps to focus attention.

(Above) "The Storming of Badajos" included a half-buried French soldier, an idea borrowed from a vignette by Steve Warrilow in 1988.

(Left & below)
"A Soldier's Battle: Inkerman, 1854".

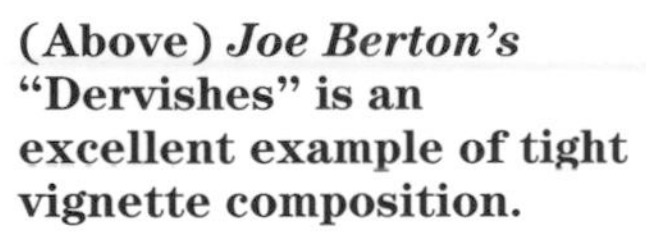

(Above) *Joe Berton's* "Dervishes" is an excellent example of tight vignette composition.

(Above right) In "The Battle of the Pyramids", *Joe Berton* introduced a humorous element to the multilevel composition of this well animated scene.

(Right) "Rebels" by *Roland Laffert* made good use of the many commercially available spare parts for American Civil War figures, particularly those from Shenandoah Miniatures.

(Right) "Three Cheers for Her Majesty" was something of an experiment in style. Note the tall, thin physiques of the figures, which were deliberately patterned on the style of period paintings by Dighton and Dubois Drahonet.

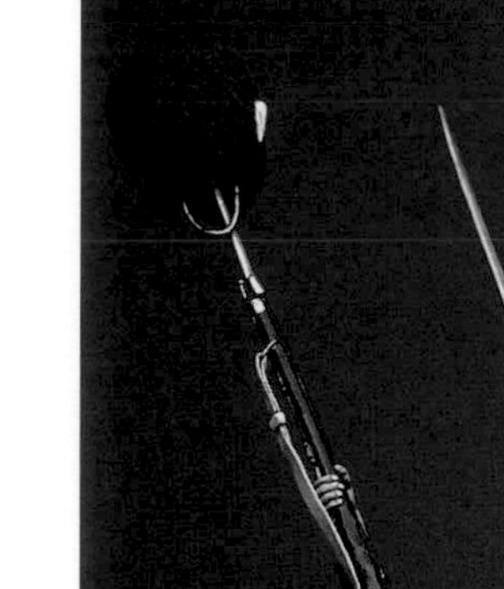

(Opposite) The author's 54mm diorama "The Ghosts of Chillianwallah".

(Below) "The Home-coming" was a bitter-sweet vignette from 1987: this cheerful soldier father has lost his left arm in the Crimea.

(Below) *Andrei Koribanics'* flamboyant and rousing "Think of England!" was a gold medal winner at the 1993 World Model Soldier Exposition; it is a superb example of economical composition, combining with colour to create an exciting vignette.

CHAPTER 4

DIORAMAS

If the vignette is a short story, then the diorama is the novel of the military miniature hobby.

Given its greater size and complexity, it is even more critical that a central focus be identified and established in the scene. The dioramas that work best are those in which the viewer's eyes are drawn to a strong "centre" that keys the scene. Other elements are typically little more than supporting window dressing - albeit important window dressing.

The enormous amount of time needed to complete major dioramas means that they are less frequently seen at miniature exhibitions. More to our point, the time needed to complete them frequently leads the miniaturist into a gradual but fatal loss of interest in the details of the scene, particularly in terms of consistent attention to figure anatomy and careful painting. Getting the details right is no less important in a diorama than it is in any other miniature project. The difference between dioramas and other lesser projects is that painting and sculpting are not the only challenges.

Selecting the right subject for a diorama is extremely important, and an avid interest in history can be a great help in this. Several years ago I was captivated by a very moving account of the 24th Regiment's attack on a Sikh position during the Battle of Chillianwallah in the Punjab during the Second Sikh War of 1848-49, as described by Byron Farwell in his fine book *Queen Victoria's Little Wars*.

In stifling heat, the regiment gallantly assaulted a position held by superior enemy numbers in dense jungle; and after briefly taking the position, despite horrendous casualties, were forced to withdraw by a counterattack. The account of this action was filled with poignant and fascinating individual stories, all of which led to a diorama entitled **"The Ghosts of Chillianwallah".** The diorama was designed to tell the story not of the attack, but of the physical and psychological cost to these British soldiers, dramatised by their appearance as survivors made their way back to their lines after the attack's failure.

Once again, a strong central focus was conceived, in this case the figure of an ageing colour-sergeant carrying back the body of the young drummer boy. The savagery of the fighting is expressed in their distressed clothing, the faces of the wounded men, and the wounds they have suffered.

RESEARCHING THE DIORAMA

The reference material needed to depict the dress worn by the 24th at Chillianwallah was derived from eyewitness accounts and pictorial evidence summarized in Michael Barthorp's Osprey Men-at-Arms book, MAA 193 *The British Army on Campaign 1816-1902.(1) 1816-1853*. It is therefore not necessary to go into much detail here. Suffice it to say that the 24th went into battle wearing their dress coatees, red with grass green collars and cuffs, and Indian-made cotton "nankeen" dungaree trousers of a blueish grey shade. The Albert shako was worn with a locally acquired white quilted cover extending over the front and rear peaks. Aside from the cartridge box and bayonet crossbelts the only item of equipment carried was the haversack, containing rations, worn over the right shoulder. The weapon carried by the rank and file was the 1842 pattern percussion rifle; and the coatee had a slit pocket just above the fourth row of lace on the right side for carrying percussion caps (sergeants had a flap pocket in roughly the same location). Native dress was very simple, and was reproduced from various contemporary paintings and sketches.

STAGE MANAGEMENT

The scene itself is designed not simply to show the exhaustion and pain felt by the survivors as they return from the battle, but also to represent the support, assistance and concern shown by their Indian servants. The interaction of Briton and

(Far left) In-process rear view of the double figure of the colour-sergeant carrying the wounded drummer boy, forming the foreground focal point of the diorama. Note the boy's hand sculpted grasping the sergeant's waist sash.

(Left) The double figure completed and painted. The boy's shoeless foot was almost an afterthought, but adds a degree of poignant vulnerability. Note the colour-sergeant's right sleeve badge; and the contrast between the shades of the NCO's and other ranks' red coats.

Indian is a subject that has always intrigued me, and one that I would have liked to depict in my Gandamak diorama; unfortunately, on that occasion all of the Indian troops and followers were gone by the time of the 44th Regiment's last stand. The aftermath of the 24th's attack at Chillianwallah provided a good opportunity to tell something of that story.

The base selected for the diorama was made by modeller/base-maker extrordinaire Phil Kessling from English brown oak, and measured 5¼ins. x 7ins. x 1¾ins.; the height included a 1in. pedestal to which was attached a "brown brass" engraved nameplate. The front of the diorama is on the narrow end (5¼ins.), so the base was cut with the grain showing on the ends rather than the long sides. This arrangement was necessary due to the processional nature of the scene.

The actual composition was greatly influenced by the paintings of Robert Gibb *(Thin Red Line; Forward, 42nd!*, etc.), in that it shows a line of soldiers travelling over undulating ground. This, coupled with the sloping nature of the base, served to show all of the figures to best advantage.

FIGURE NOTES

Colour-sergeant with drummer boy:

As can be seen from the accompanying photographs, these two figures were sculpted as one. The colour-sergeant's head is from the Hornet range, with resculpted eyes, brow (to add a bit more "sorrow") and hair. Torso sections and shoes are resin castings from my masters. All details are fashioned in Duro, with sheet plastic crossbelts. The sergeant's version of the 1822 pattern officer's sword was made by shortening a Historex scabbard and resculpting the guard. All scabbard ornaments were simply painted on, highlighting serving to suggest relief. The sword knot was made from sheet lead, with a Duro tassel.

The drummer boy was almost totally sculpted

from scratch. Only the head, pirated from an Andrea Miniatures kit, was from stock, although the hair was added. The bare foot was carved from an AM shoe, as was the shoe. The portion of the short-sword belt that extends away from the body was fashioned from sheet lead and joined to the body at the belt plate.

Private assisting wounded soldier:
As with the above figures, these were also sculpted as one, a pin under each armpit serving to hold them together throughout the process. Note the angles of the torso, legs and head - very important in depicting the weight of the wounded man on the other private's shoulder. (Inspiration came from watching a traveller struggling to carry a very heavy suitcase at an airport; I posed in the mirror with my own weighted suitcase to make sure I got it right!) The wounded man's head is a smiling Scale Link head, with resculpted eyes and brows to create the grimace; the other man's head is by Hornet.

The shako was created by first adding a thin blob of putty to the top of the head. After it dried the shape of the shako was formed around it from Duro, making it deliberately too tall. The shako was then sliced down to the correct height after it dried. Peaks were roughly formed from Duro, special care being taken to make the top surfaces accurate and smooth. The underside edge was then sliced after drying to give a sharp edge. The cover was then created by adding a thin layer of Duro into which a subtle quilted "grid" was sculpted with a sharpened toothpick.

Tears were made in the clothing while the putty was wet by slicing the knife under the surface of the torn area, and working it open to the correct position. The newly exposed areas (knee, elbow, etc.) were then smoothed.

Private carrying Regimental Colour:
This figure represents Private Perry, who returned with the Regimental Colour. As the colour party had died in a hail of grapeshot and volley fire, I felt it reasonable to assume that the staff of the colour was broken in the battle; the colour is depicted as it might have been carried after having been ripped away from the broken staff. The colour was sculpted entirely from White (fine grain) A&B putty, similar to Milliput but softer in its early stages. This was necessary, as I needed to be able to brush out the gentle draping on the colour. No details were sculpted on the colour, these being painted on later to suggest slight relief.

Indian boy carrying drum:
The Indian boy was imagined to be a concerned friend of the fallen drummer boy carried by the colour-sergeant, whose drum he has recovered. The face and sandaled feet came from the Hornet Israeli woman kit. This figure, as well as all other Indians in the diorama, was intentionally sculpted

to appear more slender and wiry than the British soldiers; a review of contemporary paintings revealed this to be a general trend. Most of the body was sculpted with White A&B, brushed out to give a smooth surface. Turban and *dhoti* were from Duro.

The drum was, of course, a Historex part, although the drum shell edges went through the cords, badly distorting them. This made it necessary to extensively resculpt a portion of the cording.The drum design is fairly typical of the period, and included a half shell in facing colour, Royal coat of arms, ten battle honour scrolls (Cape of Good Hope, Nivelle, Orthes, Salamanca, Talavera, Pyrenees, Fuentes d'Onor, Peninsula, Egypt, Vittoria), and a scroll with the regimental number and name. The hoop design is speculative, but follows a later regimental drum pattern.

Regimental bhisti:

The *bhisti* is based on a contemporary sketch, and wears typical native garb, in this case dyed to two shades of khaki. Waist sashes were very common. The water vessel was apparently made from animal skin, and is also taken from contemporary pictorial references. Note the Indian slippers.

Officer's bearer:

The dress of this diminutive figure was taken from a panorama painting of a regiment on the march in

The private assisting a wounded comrade, another challenging vignette within the diorama. Supporting much of the weight of a fainting adult puts a considerable strain on even a strong man. The angles of the shoulders and pelvis were determined partly by watching a man carry a very heavy suitcase through an airport! The effect of the quilted shako cover proved surprisingly tricky to achieve, as described in the text.

(Above & above right) The figure of Private Perry, who was promoted for rescuing the Regimental Colour; I decided to show the shot-torn flag ripped from its staff and draped across his shoulder. Battle honours and other devices were painted freehand.

(Opposite, left) The fate of the drum was a matter of interest to me in composing the scene, and this idea for its recovery offered an opportunity to introduce some added emotion: the drum is carried back by an Indian boy bearer, imagined as a friend of the wounded English drummer boy. The designs on Victorian period British Army drums followed a well-documented pattern; all that is needed is a bit of research, a good sharp brush - and a lot of time....The sling cords were added after painting.

(Opposite, right) The boy bearer set in the completed diorama, at an angle suggesting that he is trying to peer around the colour-sergeant for a glimpse of his fallen friend, thus visually establishing their relationship

India during this general period. A Peddinghaus head was used, to which were added resculpted eyes, brow, moustache, whiskers and turban. The left hand was scratchbuilt, and the right was taken from a Hornet figure. The feet were from the old Phoenix "Urchin boy" kit (sculptured by Saunders). Note again the subtle angles of the head, torso and legs to simulate the movement.

Wounded private leading blinded corporal:

These two figures were basically sculpted separately, although the blind man's left hand was sculpted onto the back of the private's shoulder. The private's "pork-pie" forage cap was a real pain to make - that shown in the photograph was the result of my third attempt! The regimental numerals and the grenade badge of the grenadier company were made from Duro, as was the peak, which was permitted for other ranks while serving in India after 1835. The loose sleeve was made from sheet lead, with White A&B brushed over it for added strength. Both heads were from the first Scale Link bare head set.

Mounted officer:

The horse used is a combination of the bare Andrea (body and tail) and Puchala (neck and head) horses. The head provided with the Andrea kit looked a bit odd to me; the Puchala head was much better, and the drooping angle gave the horse

a more sombre attitude, consistent with the scene. All horse equipment was made from Duro and/or A&B putty, with some plastic and Historex parts thrown in.

The officer depicted is not a "mounted" officer *per se*, but rather a foot officer being carried back to his lines on a stray horse. I preferred to depict a foot officer mainly because the crossbelt and plate set against his undress shell jacket made him more interesting than he would otherwise have looked in mounted order (waist belt and slings for sword, spurs). He was sculpted after, and painted separately from, the horse, but was repeatedly trial-fitted throughout his construction. The figure, stirrups, and reins were added after both horse and figure were painted and assembled.

PRIMING & PAINTING

The figures were all primed using Floquil grey metal primer. For those modellers concerned about the effects of this primer on plastic figures, a bit of explanation is needed. I have never had any problem using this primer on my conversions, which as you can see contain very little plastic; but even where the primer contacts the plastic, I have never experienced any detrimental effects. What WILL damage the plastic is the Dio-Sol thinner recommended for this primer, and great care should be taken in its use. I have found that ordinary paint thinner is perfectly satisfactory for use with Floquil primer, and I use this whenever extensive thinner contact with plastic is anticipated.

The figures were painted almost entirely with Humbrol matt enamels. However, I have found it increasingly effective to mix oil paint with the enamels to obtain certain effects, as described below. In painting the figures it was my goal to create a sense of what the soldiers had endured prior to and during the attack. For this reason it was necessary to show them to be fatigued, dusty (from the march), wounded, and with varying degrees of suntans. The most important element in creating this impression was the realistic "weathering" of the figures.

This was accomplished by working several different earth tones into the clothing while the paint was still wet, to discolour it. Colours such as Natural Wood, Flesh and Burnt Umber oil paint were dabbed into the wet blue of the trousers and reds of the coatees. Each item of clothing was then shaded, with great care being taken to ensure that the shadow colours were consistent with the discoloured areas on the clothing. In other words, the dusty lower trousers were shaded with a dark blueish brown colour, as opposed to the cleaner upper trousers which were simply shaded with various dark blues. Highlights were mixed and applied according to the same principle.

After the clothing was completed, more earth

tones were added to key points (knees, ends of trouser legs). It is very important that figures be weathered from the early stages of painting: so often one sees figures painted as if on a parade ground, with cursory dry-brushed soil added almost as an afterthought. Soldiers frequently go for long periods of time without changing clothes, and with the demands of the march, rain, dust and the rigours of battle, clothing must have become discoloured very quickly indeed.

Red coats:

The brick red coatees worn by the other ranks in the diorama were painted with a mixture of Humbrol Scarlet, Chestnut Brown, German Purple and Natural Wood. Shadows were varying mixtures of German Purple, Black, Red and Alazarin Crimson oil paint, with care being taken to balance the mixture so that the oil paint gave the colours luster without a glossy sheen. Actually, I find that a bit of a sheen in the darker shadows is okay, provided it isn't in a position to catch the light when being viewed. It gives the painting more depth, and enhances the impression of three-dimensionality.

The officer's and sergeant's scarlet shell jacket and coatee were painted similarly, but without Chestnut Brown, and with a bit of Hardened Leather substituted for the Natural Wood. This helped to give them a slightly brighter look consistent with the superior quality of their garments. Highlights were created by adding Flesh and a little Hardened Leather (MC27) to the basic colour. These colours are intentionally mixed to give the figure a duller, dustier look, consistent with his environment. Grass green collars and cuffs were mixed from Humbrol Yellow and Prussian Blue oil paint which, surprisingly enough, dried quite matt. Shadows were mixed by adding more blue and a touch of black, while highlights were mixed by adding Flesh.

All the lace on the figures was painted on (not sculpted). This was done by carefully painting in each bar with a white colour, diluted with Natural Wood and a bit of black. A paper-thin pure white highlight (clearly contrasting, or it won't be noticed) was run along the top edge, and a dark crimson shadow run along the bottom edge, creating the impression of relief. The same techniques were used when painting the belts.

The drummer's lace pattern for the 24th Foot was found in C.C.P.Lawson's notes in the National Army Museum Reading Room: white, with diagonal red dashes evenly spaced along the centre of the lace. (Someone should really make a decal for this...)

Pewter buttons were painted with a mixture of silver and gloss black; and brass belt plates were done with Rose Bright Gold powder applied over an undercoat of gloss black/copper. This gives the gold a very fine, even look. Brass/gilt was shaded with Burnt Umber oil paint, with a bit of black added for darker shadows.

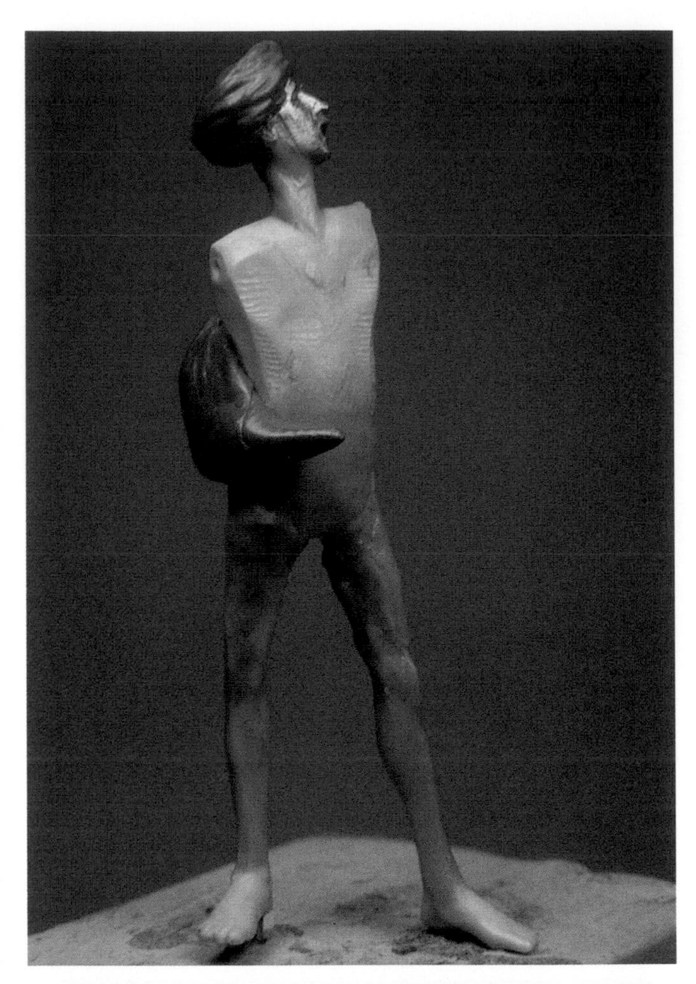

Covered shakos:

Painting the white quilted covers on the Albert shakos was a surprisingly difficult process. I found that I had an instinctive desire to paint shadows in between the squares. I continually made these shadows too dark, making the crevices in the quilting look like canyons. I ultimately settled on a subtler approach. The shakos were first undercoated in an off-white colour (white with tiny amounts of Natural Wood and black). Once dry, the top halves of each square were carefully painted with a highlight colour - NOT pure white, but close. This was then blended downward only, leaving the top edge sharp. A pure white final highlight was applied to the apex of each square, blended DOWNWARD, and a very subtle shadow colour was applied to the bottom of each square and blended UPWARD. The shakos were very time consuming to paint, each taking about two hours. However, the results proved worth the effort.

Trousers:

The cotton "nankeen" dungaree trousers worn by the 24th were painted by first applying an undercoat mixed from Prussian Dragoon Blue and small portions of Natural Wood, Prussian Blue and black oil paint. Once dry, the shadows were derived from the same colours, but with more and more Prussian Blue oil paint and black being added in the darker shadows (and less Natural Wood).

(Top left & right) The initial posing of the regimental *bhisti* or water-carrier, showing the waterskin formed under his right arm; and the figure completely sculpted, ready for priming.

(Bottom left & right) The *bhisti* painted; and set in the diorama, handing a cup of water to the mounted officer.
At right foreground can be seen the other Indian figure, the officer's bearer, leading his horse.

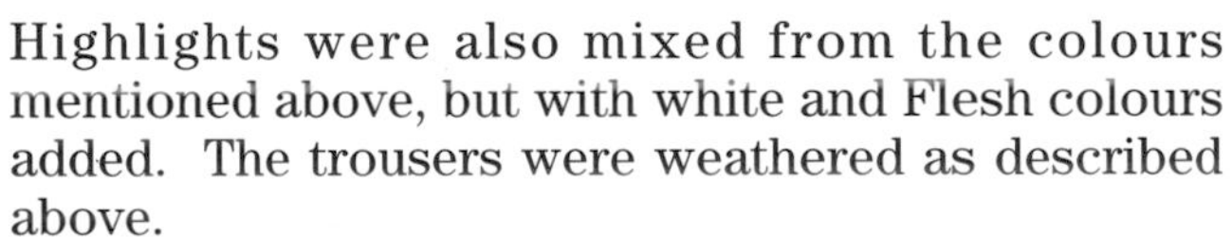

Highlights were also mixed from the colours mentioned above, but with white and Flesh colours added. The trousers were weathered as described above.

Rifles:

These were undercoated with a mixture of black, red and Hardened Leather. Once dry, a very subtle grain was added with streaks of black/red, which were then partially blended by dragging a brush moistened with thinner over the surface. The wood was then given a sheen using a combination of Polly S water-based clear flat and gloss finishes. The gunmetal barrels were painted with Humbrol Metalcote Polished Steel. Next, the top edges of the stock (the portion along each side of the barrel) were given a thin, carefully painted highlight of red/Hardened Leather/black, to visually separate the stock from the barrel. Fittings were first painted black, then detailed with silver/gloss black, shaded with black/Prussian Blue oil paint, and highlighted with pure silver. Brass fittings were painted as described for belt plates (above).

Faces:

These were painted to show varying degrees of exposure to the sun. As everyone's skin reacts differently to the sun, each of the figures was given a slightly different complexion, from the relatively dark tan of the veteran colour-sergeant to the paler complexion of the private wearing the forage cap.

Each face was undercoated with Humbrol Flesh mixed with small amounts of Natural Wood, German Purple, and Hardened Leather, the latter being the main colour for more tanned complexions. Shadow colours were primarily combinations of Hardened Leather/WWI Purple (light shadows); Hardened Leather/red/black (intermediate shadows); and red/black (dark shadows). Additional shades were created by thinning these mixtures, all of which were applied in very thin form, working from light to dark. Highlights were created by adding varying amounts of white to the basic flesh mixture. The "five-o'clock shadow" was a mixture of Natural Wood and black, applied in a very thin coat over lighter areas and more opaquely in shaded areas. Each face was given a final coat of Polly S gloss/flat clear mixture to create the impression of perspiration.

CREATING THE GROUNDWORK

The first and most important step in constructing the groundwork for the diorama was to decide upon the elevations of each of the figures in relation to each other. The figures had been roughly arranged during their construction, but at this stage the final specific locations were decided upon. As mentioned earlier, the "raked" nature of

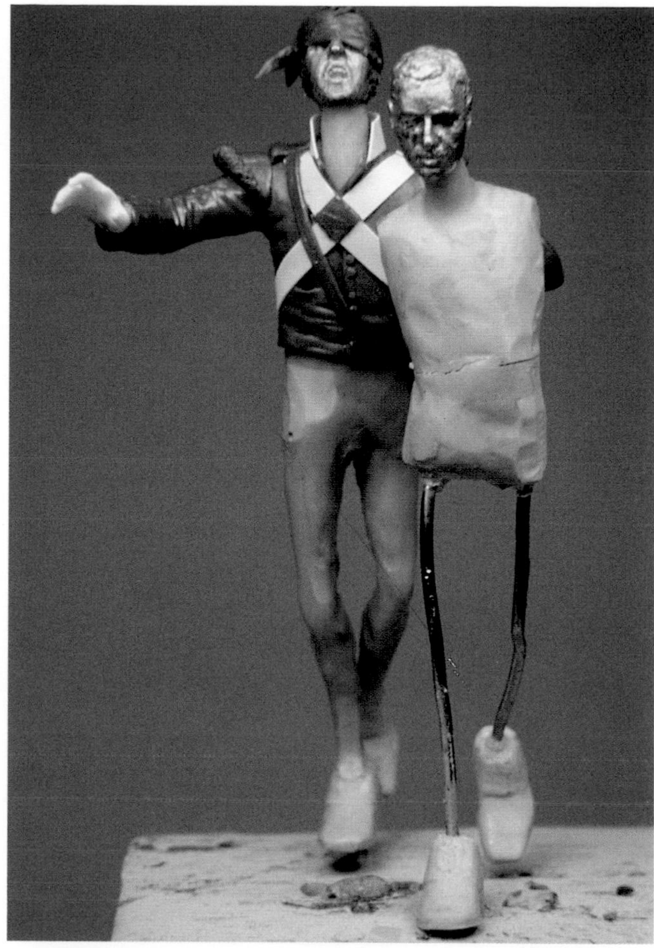

(Opposite, left) After the initial posing of the blinded corporal, a lump of Pres-Stik - equivalent to Blu-Tack - was used to prop up the delicate ends of his knotted head bandage to prevent it sagging while drying in a low oven. Note the angle of the head.

(Opposite, right) The sculpting of the blinded man continues. Note collar and crossbelts added from .010 gauge plastic sheet, and a stock Airfix Multipose hand.

(Above left) Sculpting of the blinded man is complete; his left hand would be sculpted directly onto the shoulder of the soldier leading him, the two figures being joined through the wrist.

(Above) While work was continuing on the blinded man, his comrade was begun; this was necessary to ensure a sound composition and the proper positioning of the blinded man's left arm.

(Right) New hair and downcast eyes have been added to the wounded soldier, and a wrist sling fashioned from stretched Duro. The correct shape for the crown of the forage cap was achieved by adding a bit of A&B, brushed out with Dio-Sol thinners, over a basic shape formed from Duro. Sheet lead was used for the free-hanging right sleeve.

the groundwork was designed to raise the figures toward the back of the scene, thus making them easier to see from the front of the diorama.

Quarter-inch balsa wood strips were carefully cut and glued one upon another to form the general configuration of the groundwork. I selected balsa wood for its lightness, knowing that the other elements in the groundwork would be comparatively heavy. Once the glued balsa wood had dried, strips of sheet plastic were cut to provide a crisp, sharp edge to each of the sides. These were glued in place using superglue. A&B putty was then applied throughout the surfaces of the terrain to create the contour of the groundwork, solidify the plastic borders, and provide a solid base into which the pin holes could be drilled for the figures. Several layers of putty were applied in this manner until the basic contours of the groundwork were created.

Holes were then drilled, and each figure was trial -fitted. Once the desired positioning was finalized, more A&B putty was contoured under each foot to ensure that the figures' feet met the ground properly. A layer of Spackle was smoothed over the surfaces to ease the sharp transitions in the putty. After this had dried, a very thin final coat of Cell-U-Clay (papier mache), mixed with white glue to prevent pooling, was added, into which dirt and pebbles were sprinkled. Each figure was reinserted to ensure proper attachment.

The soil was painted with various combinations of Natural Wood, Unbleached Linen, black, and Burnt Umber oil paint. The soil that would be under the denser jungle foliage was painted the darkest, the lightest area being the pathway in the centre of the base. While the paint was still wet, static grass was lightly sprinkled over the surfaces to represent trampled grass. Later, white glue was spread irregularly over the terrain in patches, onto which thicker concentrations of static grass were applied. This was initially painted a dark greenish-brown colour. Next, clumps of a grassy moss were glued mostly over the areas to be covered by the denser jungle foliage. The final stage in painting the groundwork prior to applying the plant life was to subtly dry-brush the soil and moss with light browns and greens. It should be emphasized that this was done very subtly, stark contrasts being carefully avoided.

Vegetation was made from a variety of dried flowers and plants obtained from the local arts and crafts shop, most coming in a fairly blueish green colour. These were dry-brushed with a yellowish green to make them appear more moist and... well,"jungly"! Those plants that were not green to begin with were given a heavy wash of a mixture of Prussian Blue oil paint and Humbrol yellow, and dry brushed with yellow green. All plants were given a final light spray of DEFT semi-gloss wood finish to enhance the appearance of moisture.

(Left to right:)
Rear view showing the arrangement of the equipment, and the hanging sleeve; note the hand of the wounded corporal sculpted to the right shoulder.

The pair of figures completed and painted. Small vignettes like this not only make good points of interest within larger dioramas, but are perfectly capable of standing alone as separate models.

The figures of the blinded and wounded soldiers set in their final position.

(Below left) The officer's horse was a conversion using an Andrea Miniatures body, a Puchala head, and scratch-built furniture and equipment.

(Below right) The initial posing of the officer included a trial fit into the saddle. The cone shape on the top of the head will act as a foundation for the Albert shako.

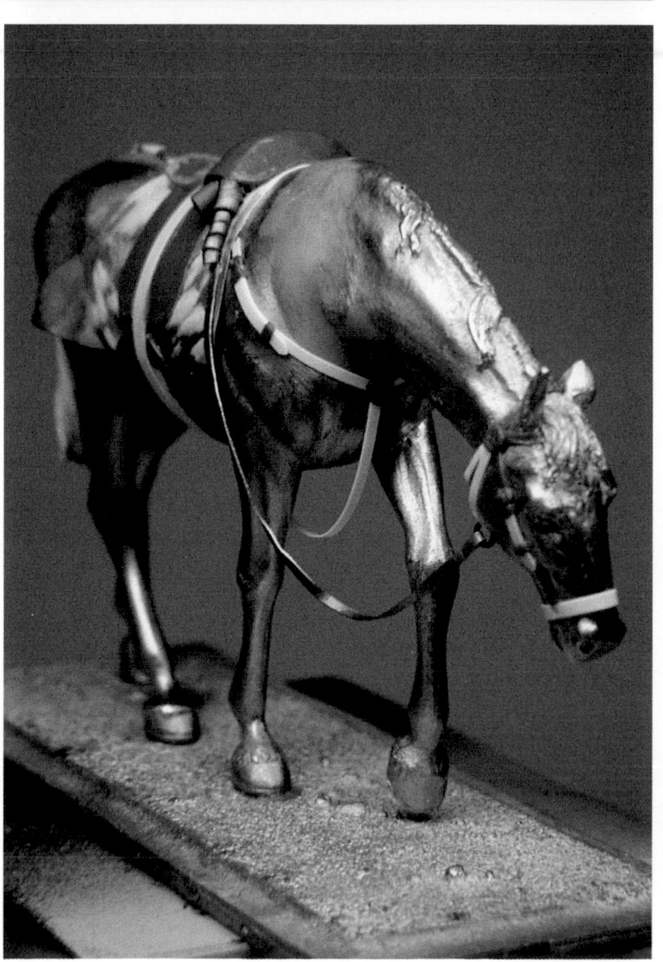

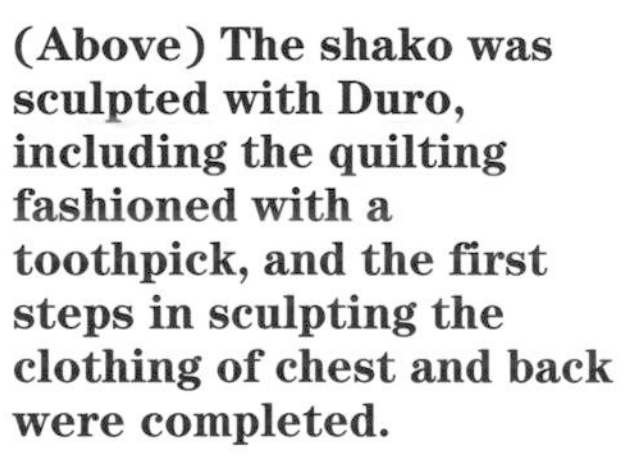

(Above) The shako was sculpted with Duro, including the quilting fashioned with a toothpick, and the first steps in sculpting the clothing of chest and back were completed.

(Above right) The sculpting of the officer completed apart from the sword and the fingers of the left hand, which will be added after painting and attachment of the horse and rider. The two sections of .010 plastic sheet forming the sword belt are mated under the shoulder knot.

(Right) The officer painted, and set in context with the *bhisti*.

Foliage was glued to the base using white glue, varying the concentrations of any one plant. Bits of Fichus root were given a green wash and randomly affixed throughout the scene, mostly protruding into view from the bushes.

It should be noted that no photo-etched brass plants were used. I found these looked very artificial in comparison with the other plants, and their flat, rigid appearance stood out in a rather unflattering way. (Besides, it was just plain easier to use the dried flowers.) The tree trunks were cut from the roots of a Fichus tree, and given either green or dark brown washes. Holes were then drilled into the trunk, into which dried flower branches were inserted and attached with superglue.

The swampy area in the left front corner of the base was created simply by painting the bare wood of the base with various brown colours, and coating with three coats of Fiberglass resin. (Polyester resin would have worked as well, but I couldn't find any at the local hardware stores.)

Cannon balls were made from rolled putty, and painted with Humbrol black and Natural Wood. Finally, the figures were inserted into their respective holes in the base and glued with five-minute epoxy.

(Above right) Rear view of the completed diorama showing some of the jungle foliage, most of which was made from natural dried plants. The exposed groundwork was thinly covered with static grass or moss to give an overall effect of the matted, fibrous texture of the jungle floor.

(Right) "The Ghosts of Chillianwallah" - the focal group of figures in close-up.

"Last Stand at Gandamak": on 13 January 1842, in the final grisly drama of the disastrous British retreat from Kabul to Jellalabad during the First Afghan War, the last handful of survivors of the 44th (East Essex) Regiment sell their lives dearly on an icy hillside. A six-month project which took approximately 500 hours' work in all, "Gandamak" gradually took on a life of its own. Initially the author had planned for the diorama to consist of eight to ten figures, the six central figures around Captain Souter (with the colours wrapped round his waist under his Afghan coat) forming the focus. It escalated to a final count of 27 figures. (Best of Show, 1988 Euro-Militaire and Chicago Show)

(Right & above) Again, many of the single figures and "vignettes" within the Gandamak diorama, virtually inivisible to the casual observer, would have made compelling subjects for models in their own right.

(Left & below) In vignettes and dioramas - as in reality on 19th century battlefields - regimental colours make ideal focal points, their intricate and colourful detail and commanding height drawing the observer's eye naturally. The colours carried here, those of the British 24th Foot in the Sikh Wars, were made from sheet lead. Battle honour scrolls and other details were sculpted on the surface in Duro, and painted with enamels; note the highlighting and shadowing effects. Undulations in the silk were made after painting was completed by *gently* bending the flags by hand. In fact, the author now finds rolled-out A&B putty a superior medium for flags of this type; its flexibility allows for more elaborate and realistic draping.

CHAPTER 5

MOUNTED FIGURES & DIORAMAS

When done well, a diorama featuring mounted cavalrymen is among the most thrilling images in the hobby. The best mounted scenes combine action and motion with colour and a touch of flair.

During the 1970s, demonstrating mastery of the 54mm mounted figure was almost a right of passage for up-and-coming miniaturists. Such well-known names as Sheperd Paine, Ray Lamb, Peter Twist, Ray Anderson, Andrei Koribanics, Max Longhurst and many others pioneered the fine art of converting Historex figures from the stiff, mannequin-like forms in which they emerged from the packaging into vital, animated miniatures - and collected trophies and accolades along the way. Today, miniaturists like Greg DiFranco, Martin Livingstone, Jean-Pierre Duthilleul, Philippe Gengembre and Bill Ottinger continue the tradition of the Historex conversion, taking it to new heights.

Despite the obvious attraction of mounted conversions, the fact remains that they are very time-consuming, and often tedious if one is determined to achieve a high level of quality in their completion. Hooves must be hollowed out and detailed; bridles designed and ornamented; saddlery scratchbuilt (for all except French Napoleonic subjects); horse bodies thickened, and some sort of realistic mane and tail created. Once again, careful planning, sound research and a tireless attention to detail are imperative. What is also needed is stamina.

Historex figures can take a long time to complete, and for many miniaturists boredom sets in, resulting in a corresponding lapse in quality. The challenges are many, but the rewards are potentially great. Completing a successful Historex mounted conversion or diorama remains one of the more satisfying experiences in the hobby.

The subject of this chapter is the creation of a vignette entitled (from a descriptive quotation) **"A Cloud of Red"**, depicting three charging soldiers of the British 16th Lancers as they would have appeared at the Battle of Aliwal on 16 January 1846 during the First Sikh War. On that day the regiment made a series of famous charges, distinguishing themselves in fierce fighting against enemy irregular cavalry, guns, and particularly against strong, formed-up units of disciplined infantry. Although victorious they paid a high price: 89 all ranks dead or mortally wounded and 53 other wounded - total casualties equal to 27% of the regiment's pre-battle strength. (A detailed account of the action by Michael Barthorp, with uniform colour plates by the late Rick Scollins, will be found in *Military Illustrated* magazine No.43/December 1991, which at the time of this writing was still available from the publishers.)

***"A Cloud of Red: The Charge of the 16th Lancers at Aliwal, 1846"*- 54mm vignette by the author.**

THE COMPOSITION

As with all vignettes and dioramas, the key to success is to select a strong central focus, in this case the officer on the dapple grey in the centre of the group. His lunging pose, out-thrust sabre, and dapple grey horse were all calculated to focus the viewer's attention. For added interest, the central figure's horse was suspended from a wire pin which doubled as the right arm of the wounded sergeant to his left, creating the illusion that the horse is floating in mid-leap. Again, once the central figure was established as the focus, the balance of the scene was designed around him.

The officer was the first part of the vignette to be sculpted, and this was done using the same basic principles as described in preceding chapters. The pose was finalized only after trial-fitting it over the

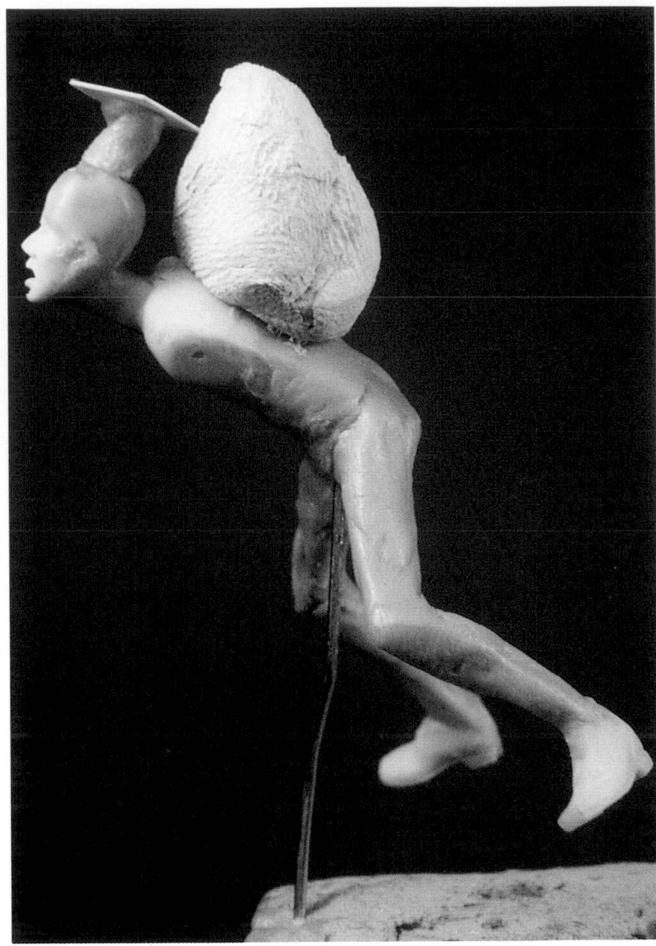

roughly formed horse, to ensure a good secure fit for the legs. The head selected was the Historex "open mouth" variant. While this head has much potential the detailing leaves something to be desired, and extensive reworking was necessary to create the required intensity in this crucial figure's facial features. The forehead and brow, eyes, nose, teeth and facial hair were all sculpted from scratch using Duro putty.

The lance cap was formed through a series of planned stages, beginning with the establishment of the basic silhouette, continuing through the "fleshing out" of the cap body, to the final addition of the cover and details. Although an assortment of materials are available to use as cap lines - the cords which keep the headgear from being lost during a charge - I chose to make them from thinly rolled Duro "strings".

The figure was sculpted in stages, beginning with the collar, chest and back, left arm, right arm, and so on. As the clothing was added care was taken to consider the belting to be added later and the affect it would have on the folds in the clothing. The pouch belt was of particular concern, and a "channel" into which the belt would fit was made by slightly impressing the belt into the wet putty. Near the shoulder area, where the belt's weight would be most apparent, the indentation was most noticeable; other portions of the jacket with which the belt would come in contact were simply smoothed over to keep the belt from "perching" on them. Once the putty

(Above left) The initial posing of the central figure in *"A Cloud of Red"*. Note the angle of the head and pivoting of the upper torso. The spacing of the legs was based on a trial fit on the horse.

(Above) The crown of the lance cap is sculpted, and the top of the cap crudely attached with a blob of putty. A large piece of Pres-Stik (Blu-Tack) holds the top of the cap in place while drying in the oven at 140F. The legs have been fleshed out with A&B epoxy putty.

(Above) The lance cap shape has been sculpted from Duro putty, and the arms formed and shaped with A&B in similar fashion to the legs.

(Above right) Reworking the face. Note the resculpted brow, with lowered eyebrows, and the squinting eyes. These features are calculated to create a sense of concentration and determination on the face of the officer. The final shape of the lance cap cover has been added from A&B putty brushed out using Dio-Sol as a medium.

(Right) The work on the face is now complete, including the sideburns, moustache, and hair curling up from beneath the cap. The nose has been given greater definition, and teeth have been added to the open mouth. The smaller details have been added to the cap.

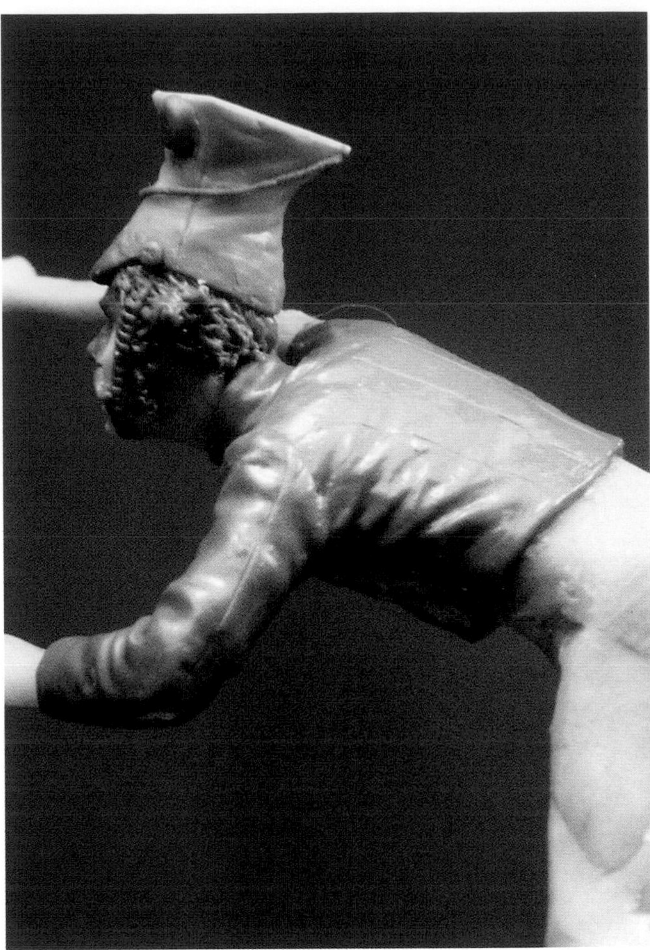

(Above & right) The jacket in process. The Duro putty is particularly well suited to this type of work. The tight folds in the sleeves and the subtle wrinkling in the jacket body were easily sculpted with a round toothpick.

was dry on the chest, the pouch belt - carefully cut from sheet plastic in an arc to ensure a good fit around the body - was superglued in place. Fittings and ornaments were added from Duro.

Uniform details such as buttons, lace and buckles were sculpted from Duro putty, sliced in very small balls, applied with the tip of a toothpick, and detailed with an X-Acto knife. Any difficulties in getting these very small objects to stick to the figure were overcome by carefully dipping the piece in a bit of superglue prior to application. Trousers were sculpted one leg at a time, and regularly trial-fitted to the horse to ensure the proper fit was maintained.

Among the final touches applied to the officer were the spurs; and the fingers, those on the right hand grasping a sword grip without the knuckle guard, which was added after the fingers had dried using rolled-out Duro strings similar to, but thicker than the cap lines.

CONVERTING THE HORSES

The first step in converting a Historex horse is to decide upon a pose and select the appropriate horse halves. Actually, Historex horses need not simply be selected by halves, but can be further cut into quarters, greatly expanding the range of posing options available to the miniaturist. In the case of the mounted officer's horse I selected two halves with all hooves off the ground, as I had decided to make the horse appear to be in mid-air, suspended by

(Above left) Sculpting is almost completed. Sheet plastic was used for the sword and pouch belts, and stretched sprue for the cap lines wound round the body. Belt fittings were formed from Duro, as were such details as buttons, buckles and clasps.

(Above) In this front view, note the elevation of the shoulder to accommodate the thrusting right arm.

the pin in his left flank.

When attempting an in-motion conversion of a horse it is obviously important to study photographic evidence. (It is a sobering fact that before technical improvements in photography allowed "stop frame" images of galloping horses to be captured, virtually all paintings of horses in rapid motion were inaccurate: the human eye - even the eye of such a dedicated student as Stubbs - could not capture the relative positions of the fast-moving legs. Thus the "classical" depiction of horses with both front and both back legs moving more or less together.)

Before the halves could be glued together the rump of each half was sanded to a rounded shape, as the rump curves towards the inside of the flange. This is necessary, as the shim which needs to be inserted will separate the two halves enough to alter the rear of the horse. Next, the shim had to be added between the halves to thicken the horse, as Historex horses always appear a bit on the narrow side without this "beefing-up". The shim used was an old Airfix "Multi-Pose" plastic base on which the contact shape of the horse half was traced before cutting it out. This piece was then superglued to one horse half, and the other half attached afterwards. The resulting gaps were filled with A&B putty and allowed to dry.

The hooves were the next mini-project tackled. First the inside of the hoof was hollowed out using a motor tool drill, taking care not to run through the

hoof or damage the edges. Once the interior of the hoof had been hollowed out, the triangular shape was sculpted from the fetlock in accordance with a reference drawing of a horse hoof. The final touch was to add the shoes, which are (thankfully) available from Historex. Because there is some mismatch between the hooves and the shoes, the hooves were built up with A&B in some places to make them more compatible with the size of the shoe. Many miniaturists like to super-detail the horse's ankle hair just above the hoof with a hot knife. I prefer simply to define this hair with some carefully painted highlights and shadows painted in line by line. Either method will produce good results if properly executed.

The horse's head was selected from the spares box. Unfortunately I could not find a head with an open mouth; so the lower jaw of the horse was carved away, and a new one sculpted from A&B in a slightly open position. Because Historex horse heads come with a French bridle moulded to them it is necessary to remove this by carving and sanding it away, care being taken not to damage the eyes, nostrils or other details that must remain. Once the bridle was removed the ears were sculpted from A&B.

The neck was first formed from a length of sturdy paperclip wire and glued into holes drilled into the shoulder flange and the base of the horse's head, the length being carefully measured to ensure the proper proportions were obtained. Once the neck was so attached, the head was manipulated until just the proper angle was established. The neck was built up with A&B putty to about 3/4 thickness, and set aside to dry. The neck musculature and final shape were then sculpted, again using A&B putty, this time smoothed out with a brush moistened with Dio-Sol thinner. The mane and tail were added later, after completion of the horse furniture and equipment.

HORSE FURNITURE, SADDLERY & EQUIPMENT

Because the many straps comprising the bridle, halter, girth, etc., overlap and often partially obscure one another, it is very important to study reference material carefully, and to devise a step-by-step plan before embarking on this phase. The bridle straps were virtually all cut from sheet plastic and superglued in place. Ornaments on the officer's bridle, as well as buckles, were made from Duro. The same technique applied to all of the belting and strapping on the horse, as well as the saddle side panels. Teeth and tongue were sculpted into the horse's mouth from Duro.

The fact that the sheepskin covers much of the saddlery of the British Victorian cavalryman is something of a relief, in that it reduces the amount of time needed to complete this portion of the figure. The portions of the saddlery which are visible must of course be convincingly reproduced, but those hidden beneath the sheepskin need only have their shapes suggested by its visible contours.

(Far left & centre) The basic forming of the horse. Separate Historex horse halves have been glued together with a thickening "shim" inserted between them. The horse's head has been attached with wire to facilitate the sculpting of a suitable neck.

(Left & below left) The neck, lower jaw, and ears have been sculpted from A&B putty, after filling of the gap between the horse halves using A&B.

(Below) Virtually all the strapping against the horse's body was done with sheet plastic, as can be seen here. Buckles, fittings and ornaments have been added from Duro. Also well illustrated are the sheet plastic saddle side boards, and the hollowed and detailed hooves.

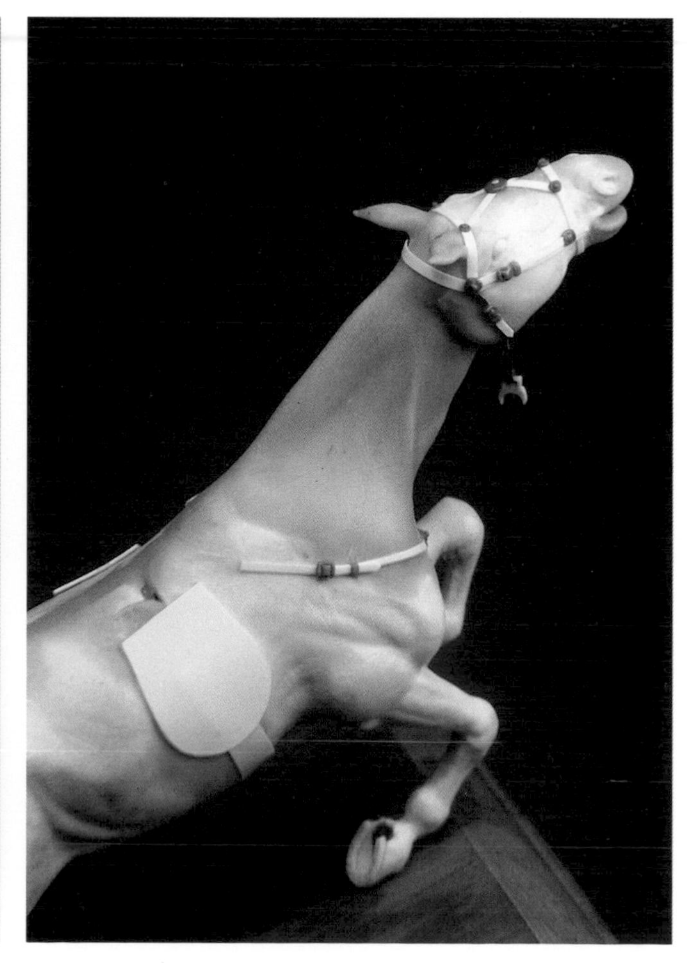

The saddle bags were formed on a flat board from Duro, and sliced off at the top after they had dried to provide a sharp edge to the top of the bag. Flaps were then made from sheet plastic superglued to the back of the bag, bent over the top, and glued against the front. Straps and buckles were once again made from sheet plastic and Duro. The rolled greatcoat was made by rolling out nearly dry A&B putty to a paper-thin consistency, after which it was cut to size and folded much as a real greatcoat might have been, and superglued in place across the front of the saddle.

Finally, the sheepskin saddle cover was sculpted from Duro and textured with an X-Acto knife. As mentioned, the contour of the sheepskin was dictated by the shape of the saddle, saddle bags, greatcoat and other objects beneath it. After the sheepskin was sculpted, and while the putty was still tacky, the figure was gently pressed into the saddle, his inner thighs moistened to prevent them from sticking to the wet putty. This ensures that the figure will fit securely in the saddle when attached later.

The mane and tail were each added at this stage from Duro putty, but using very different processes. The mane was made in three or four separate sections, each from rolled-out Duro which was then contoured by gently scribing with a toothpick and X-Acto knife. The sections created in this manner (which looked very similar to miniature Poste Militaire mane sections) were attached to the top edge of the neck. The tail was sculpted by forming a large "roll" of Duro on a paperclip wire inserted into a hole drilled where the tail attaches to the rump. The tail was then scribed and detailed using the same tools.

PAINTING THE HORSES

The large areas to be painted on the horses make the use of enamels very difficult, and I prefer to use artist oil paints. The horses were first given an undercoat in a Humbrol enamel colour similar in tone to that which the horse would be painted. After the undercoat had thoroughly dried, the various areas to which shadow and highlight colours were to be applied were identified, and the appropriate colours were applied. The remaining areas were "filled in" with a neutral mid-tone (off-white in the case of the grey, or medium golden brown for the sergeant's bay).

The transitions between each of the many shadow, highlight and mid-tone colours were blended into one another using a dry brush in a jabbing, stippling motion. This technique is far more effective than a back-and-forth stroking motion, which tends to wipe the paint away from the undercoat, leaving embarrassing brush strokes. It also has the added benefits of being faster, and leaving the horse with a coarse texture similar to that of real horse hair.

Colour selection is important. For the dapple grey, it is important to understand that the hide (or skin) of the horse is black, not the pinkish flesh colour of many other horses. For this reason, areas where the

hair is thinner tend to be a darker colour. Paler sections of the horse were mixed from a combination of white, black, and Naples Yellow, with just a bit of Burnt Umber mixed in.

All highlight and shadow colours were mixed from combinations of these colours; and care was taken to give the areas which would receive dappling a slightly darker cast, to create room for the contrast necessary to accentuate the dapple effect. Dapples were added in the form of small white dots, after the paint had begun to dry. Each dot was carefully blurred into the base colour, care being taken to blur the edges while retaining the essentially circular shape of the dapples.

Final touches included the darkening of the area around the mouth, nostrils and eyes; as well as the careful painting of the horse's eyes, allowing only a speck of "white" to show, and the glazing of the eye with a coat of clear gloss.

The bay and dark bay horses of the remaining two figures were painted using the same techniques, but different colours. The lighter bay of the sergeant was painted with a mixture of Burnt Umber, Venetian Red, Yellow Ochre and black, the yellow being primarily on the horse's belly, a feature peculiar to bay horses. The dark bay was painted with the same colours, minus the Venetian Red.

All horse furniture and equipment was painted in enamels, as were the horses' tails, manes, facial details, hooves, etc. The techniques used here are

(Above) The horse completed and ready for priming. It is supported on the working base by paperclip wire inserted into a hole drilled at the point where, in the finished miniature, the arm of the sergeant riding on the officer's left will seem to make accidental contact as he falls. The rolled greatcoat was formed by rolling out A&B putty and, when it was nearly dry, folding and rolling it up like the real thing.

(Right) The lancer private riding on the officer's right is complete and ready for priming; note his straight spine in this riding position. The gauntlets are made of sheet plastic and Duro.

(Above) The horse of the central officer is suspended in midair by a pin which doubles as the arm of the falling sergeant. The heavy paperclip wire provided sufficient support, and a good foundation on which to sculpt the sergeant's arm. Note that this is not done until after both are otherwise painted and attached. The pair would make too unwieldy a shape to handle for painting any other way.

the same as those described in previous chapters; however, it is important to emphasize a few key points.

As the strapping used by the 16th Lancers was of brown leather, a problem of contrast arose when painting these details against a brown horse. Obviously the first step is to paint the straps a colour as different as possible from that of the horse without overstepping the constraints of historical accuracy. As shades of brown leather vary greatly this is a reasonable step to take. However, the most important point in separating two similar, overlapping colours is to emphasize the highlighting along the top edge of the straps. A pale highlight carefully applied only to the top edge of the strap really works wonders, and a thin, dark (black) line running along the underside of the strap completes the effect. The final touch is to apply a coat of semi-gloss finish to the leather straps, further defining these details.

PAINTING THE FIGURES; AND FINISHING TOUCHES

The techniques used in painting the figures were almost identical to those described in Chapter 1, but added emphasis was given to the weathering of the figures. As the 16th Lancers had spent many weeks in the saddle prior to the battle, marching over very hot, dry, dusty roads, the appearance of their uniforms would undoubtedly have been very different from the pristine effect expected on the parade ground.

(Right) Close-up of the falling sergeant. The completed right arm suspension pin can be seen.

Liberal amounts of Flesh and Natural Wood were mixed with the base colours of the jackets, trousers, shoes and lance cap covers to create a suitably dusty, grimy appearance. Tiny lines of clear gloss were also added to the temples to simulate trickling perspiration, and deep red patches were painted in the armpits to further emphasize the stifling heat.

Once the figures had all been painted, they were epoxy-glued to their saddles, and final details such as reins, bits and stirrups were attached. Reins were made from sheet copper or electrical tape (the stickiness of the latter being removed with paint thinner), cut as thinly as possible, and glued to the Historex bit and hands. The reins were then primed and painted in the same manner as other straps on the horse. The suppleness of the sheet copper made it possible to form drooping reins that held their shape. The electrical tape reins were superglued to the bit, pulled taught to the rider's fingers, and superglued in place, creating a convincing sense of tension.

One of the most important steps completed at this stage was the attachment of the officer and horse to the falling sergeant. As the pin would double as the sergeant's right arm, the sergeant was painted completely and attached to his horse first, which was securely pinned to the base by a pre-drilled "channel" through the hoof and up the back of the leg to the thigh. After the pin had been glued in place the channel and pin were puttied over with A&B. Once sergeant and officer had been completely painted, they were permanently attached by glueing the pin joining the sergeant's shoulder to the left flank of the officer's horse. The arm and hand were then sculpted, brush-primed and painted.

Groundwork was formed roughly from A&B putty, particularly the sections in which the horse's hoof pins would need to be inserted. The remainder of the terrain was fleshed out with Cell-U-Clay, a papier mache product available in art stores. The soil, stones and grass were painted with Humbrol enamels.

(Below) The completed vignette from the rear; the three horses have only two of the total of twelve hooves pinned to the ground.

Close-up of the central focus of the completed vignette, and overall view.

(Left) A single figure from the same regiment: conveying a sense of the excitement and rage of battle is a challenge, and the sudden startled, angry, over-the-shoulder glance of this 16th Lancers officer, about to slash back with his sabre at the assailant who has just wounded his left arm, brings a sense of immediacy to the figure.

(Below) In-process shot of the author's heavily converted Heller camel, with scratch-built equipment, for a Guards Camel Regiment figure of the Gordon relief campaign, Sudan, 1885; and the completed miniature. Note the coarse texture of the camel, which was created by "scrubbing" the camel's base colour of yellow ochre with progressively lighter shades.

(Above) Mongol warrior by *Jim Johnston.* Jim has extensively reworked a standard horse kit to depict the smaller pony of the steppes. Note the worn look of the kaftan, and the lamellar bronze breastplate - added piece by piece from sheet plastic.

(Above right) *Bill Ottinger's* "Aide-de-Camp to General Rapp" is an excellent example of the exciting movement combined with brilliant colour which make Bill's work stand out at exhibitions.

(Right) *Michael Collins'* use of an elevated rocky outcropping helped to set off his fine Polish Lancer officer of the 1580s Russian campaign. The bear pelt horse cloth was sculpted from Duro, as was the leopardskin cape.

(Above) Major Jolly of Napoleon's Dragoons is portrayed here in all his glory by *Greg DiFranco.* Once again, horse and rider both have the same air - the dignity and formality of the parade ground.

(Above right) *Jim Johnston's* 100mm version of Major Jolly offers an interesting large-scale comparison with *Greg DiFranco's* 54mm piece. Jim made use of a Poste Militaire horse, a Verlinden head, and a great deal of putty to create this gem.

(Right) This book is devoted to military historical subjects; but we couldn't resist including *Bill Pritchard's* delightful fantasy piece, which demonstrates that there are many interesting variations on the horse-and-rider theme.

(Above) In "Revolt in the Desert", *Joe Berton* brilliantly captures the drama of a camel charge. The flying robes, banner and whip add impact and a heightened sense of movement and danger to the scene. Note also the tight grouping of the figures.
(Photo:Lane Stewart)

(Left) "Tamerlane", a 54mm Historex conversion by *G.Bibeyan*.

(Above left) *Greg DiFranco* has mastered the use of unravelled embroidery floss for horse manes and tails; this technique, coupled with his already considerable sculpting and oil painting skills, has given birth to masterpieces such as his "Scipio Africanus", a major 75mm conversion.

(Above) *Philippe Gengembre's* figure of a 15th century knight in tournament armour and barding is a superb example of oil painting large areas, coupled with intricate detail. This piece earned Philippe a Best of Show at the 1992 Euro-Militaire competition.

(Left) An exquisite example of fine horse painting by *Derek Hansen:* Metal Modeles' 54mm kit of a French Napoleonic trumpeter of the 19th Dragoons. *(Photo:Derek Hansen)*

Derek Hansen **made use of a combination of Duro and Milliput in creating his award-winning German Uhlan. Yellow electrical tape was used for some of the belting. Derek uses an unusual oil-painting technique involving layering and washes. This miniature, which won Best of Show at Euro-Militaire 1990, is an excellent example of the conversion possibilities inherent in many good kits, such as the Andrea Miniatures WWI German Lancer used here.** ***(Photos:Derek Hansen)***

(Above) "A Crash of Steel: Ramnaggar, 1848", by the author. The figures and horses are major Historex conversions. The ring-mail neck curtains worn by the Sikh cavalrymen are small pieces of nylon stocking, first painted gloss black, then detailed in silver printer's ink.

(Right) "Victory!" The author's miniature of an officer of the Royal Dragoons, in British heavy cavalry uniform of post-1812, exulting at the end of a successful engagement. Note the raised shoulder to accomodate the uplifted arm.

(Right) The author's "A Desperate Endeavor: Saving the Colour at Isandlwana" depicts the legendary - and doomed - attempt by Lieutenants Melvill and Coghill of the 24th Regiment to save the Queen's Colour of the 1st Battalion in the aftermath of the disastrous defeat at the hands of the Zulu army on 22 January 1879.

(Left) Depicting extremes of movement can be fun and exciting. The combination of the rearing horse and the precarious extension of the rider adds impact to the author's conversion of an officer of the 6th (Inniskilling) Dragoons in the Crimea, 1854.